10.36

Teaching
Cross-Culturally

San Diego Christian College
2100 Greenfield Drive
El Cajon, CA 92019

306.43
L755t
C. 3

Teaching
Cross-Culturally

An Incarnational Model for Learning and Teaching

Judith E. Lingenfelter

and

Sherwood G. Lingenfelter

 Baker Academic

A Division of Baker Book House Co
Grand Rapids, Michigan 49516

© 2003 by Judith E. Lingenfelter and Sherwood G. Lingenfelter

Published by Baker Academic
a division of Baker Book House Company
P.O Box 6287, Grand Rapids, MI 49516-6287
www.bakeracademic.com

Second printing, July 2004

Printed in the United States of America

All rights reserved. No part of this publication may be reproduced, stored in a retrieval system, or transmitted in any form or by any means—for example, electronic, photocopy, recording—without the prior written permission of the publisher. The only exception is brief quotations in printed reviews.

Library of Congress Cataloging-in-Publication Data
Lingenfelter, Judith.
    Teaching cross-culturally : an incarnational model for learning and teaching / Judith E. Lingenfelter and Sherwood G. Lingenfelter.
       p. cm.
    Includes bibliographical references and index.
    ISBN 0-8010-2620-2 (pbk.)
    1. Educational anthropology. 2. Multicultural education. 3. Teachers—Training of—Foreign countries. 4. Teaching—Religious aspects—Christianity. I. Lingenfelter, Sherwood G. II. Title.
LB45.L53 2003
306.43—dc21   2002038391

Unless otherwise indicated, Scripture is from the HOLY BIBLE, NEW INTERNATIONAL VERSION®. NIV®. Copyright © 1973, 1978, 1984 by International Bible Society. Used by permission of Zondervan Publishing House. All rights reserved.

Scripture marked KJV is from the King James Version of the Bible.

Scripture marked NLT is from the *Holy Bible*, New Living Translation, copyright © 1996. Used by permission of Tyndale House Publishers, Inc., Wheaton, IL 60189. All rights reserved.

Scripture marked NJB is from THE NEW JERUSALEM BIBLE, copyright © 1985 by Darton, Longman & Todd, Ltd. and Doubleday, a division of Bantam Doubleday Dell Publishing Group, Inc. Reprinted by permission.

To my mother, Viola Beaumont, who returned to teaching
so that I could go to college
and whose joy in her profession inspired me

and

to the many students and colleagues who have helped us
learn so much . . .
thank you!

Contents

Preface

The intended audience for this book is the western-trained educator who is working or planning to work in a non-western school setting or in a multicultural school or university in a major city of North America. We use the terms *western* and *expatriate* interchangeably, since "western-trained" may encompass North Americans, Europeans, Koreans, Japanese, and others educated to teach but who lack understanding of the cultural context of the students with whom they interact.

Whether one teaches adults or children, whether the subject matter is the Bible, English, or community development, the cultural issues and obstacles that affect teaching and learning are common to all. We, therefore, have several goals for this book. The first goal is to help teachers understand their own culture of teaching and learning. All of us are people of a culture, and we carry our cultural heritage and practices, including our practice of faith, with us into every situation of life. Unless we have a clear understanding of our cultural self and how that self restricts our acceptance of and service to others, we will not readily reach an understanding of others or be able to serve them effectively.

The second goal is to equip teachers to become effective learners in another cultural context, with specific focus on learning for teaching. Toward that end, we examine in depth the relation of culture to schooling, learning, and teaching. We also explore how schooling is part of a larger community context and how that context shapes both learning and effective teaching. Our purpose in this exploration is to help teachers adapt their thinking, relationship styles, and teaching to the understandings of others.

The third goal is to help teachers reflect on the cultural differences and conflicts they have with others using the perspectives of Scripture and faith in Jesus Christ. The Bible gives principles for living that transcend culture, but we often miss appropriate application of these principles because of cultural blindness. We, therefore, seek to discern areas of cultural blindness and explore ways to cope with that blindness when teaching and engaging in cross-cultural relationships.

The fourth goal is simple: We would like teachers working outside their home culture to enjoy their teaching experience and to feel as though they are helping to disciple the people to whom God has called them. Toward that end, we provide practical illustrations and helps from our ministries and those of others with whom we have worked.

During the past thirty years, we have worked with many colleagues in non-western contexts. While they usually received some cross-cultural orientation, that training rarely included instruction or guidance on how to teach; it was assumed that they already knew how to teach. It is to our fellow laborers in Christ that we write this book, because they have helped us to become more effective learners, teachers, and servants of the Lord Jesus Christ. We especially want to say thank you to our friends in SIL International who arranged for me (Judy) to observe classes in many places and who talked with both of us over the years about these issues. Several SIL colleagues in Thailand and some of my doctoral students at Biola provided helpful suggestions on an earlier version of the text.

Many of the examples in this book arise from personal experiences or from the experiences of colleagues. Most of our personal experiences and those of our students, Americans and internationals, took place in Bible schools and seminaries started by missionaries. Judy wrote the teaching and learning aspects of each chapter, while Sherwood wrote the biblical reflections, cultural learning tools, and applications for teaching. The use of "I" in the text always refers to Judy unless specified "I (Sherwood)."

one

Teaching Cross-Culturally

I come from a family of teachers, and I grew up knowing I would follow in the family tradition. I graduated from college with a bachelor's degree in English literature and a secondary teaching credential. My first teaching job, in a predominantly Anglo, middle-class school, while not easy, confirmed my enthusiasm for the profession. I had been well trained in college, and daily teaching reinforced my pedagogical prowess.

It was during my second teaching job that everything started to fall apart. My husband, Sherwood, had been accepted to study cultural anthropology at the University of Pittsburgh, and I landed a teaching job at a junior high school in McKeesport, Pennsylvania, a steel city south of Pittsburgh. Most of my students were African Americans or the children of second-generation Euro-American steel worker families on relief. The middle-class whites were moving out of McKeesport as quickly as they could change jobs and find a "better" school for their children. Since my student teaching had been in junior high, as had my first position, I felt that this school would be a good fit. How wrong I was! The students did not respond as I had anticipated, they did not take tests well, some were several years below their grade level, and they challenged me at every turn. I was miserable! After two years I became pregnant with our first child and thereafter only substituted until Sherwood finished his doctoral course work. I survived the experience, but I did not understand what had happened to me until several years later.

Sherwood chose the small island of Yap, in the western Pacific islands near the Philippines, to do his dissertation fieldwork. My first year there was spent learning the language and the culture, but in the second year, the American principal of the elementary school in the district center asked me if I would teach. It was November, and this particular class of twenty-four students from six different cultures had already gone through four teachers since September. The teachers had been wives of Americans based on Yap for varying lengths of time. They had not been formally trained, but they could speak English. Because the class was taught in English, it was assumed that they could handle a class of first, second, and third graders. When the assumption proved false, the principal recruited me. I had never taught elementary school, but I was at least a teacher. Maybe I would have better luck.

That experience completely changed my understanding of teaching. While I was using American textbooks and the classroom format was familiar, nothing progressed as I thought it should. Students helped one another with everything and almost never worked alone. They were personally self-sufficient, yet they tended to answer my questions as a group. The five American students in the class were routinely frustrated because things were not done "right." On the playground, the island students picked lice out of one another's hair, which the American students considered "gross." In the classroom, the American students raised their hands to answer questions, which the Yapese students thought was silly.

Nothing, however, revealed the differences between an American classroom and this Yapese one more than the incident that occurred during the final week of school. On Monday I had gone to school not feeling well but had listed on the board all the things we had to do as a class to get ready to close the school for the year (there were no janitors or other staff; the teachers were responsible for their own rooms). On Tuesday I decided I just could not make it to school. Because there were no phones and thus there was no way to contact the principal, I hoped he would notice that my students were locked out of their classroom and would send them home (substitute teachers were also an unknown commodity). About 9:00 A.M. he unlocked the classroom so that they could wait inside just in case I had been delayed by the bad roads or unreliable transportation. He then promptly forgot about them until 10:30. He went over to lock the classroom only to find the entire class diligently cleaning up and checking off the tasks on the board. Stunned, he said to the class, "You can all go home because obviously Mrs. Judy isn't going to be here today." Their response? "We can't go; we're not finished yet!" When I heard this story the next morning, I was dumbfounded by the comparison between this class and those I had previously taught. I had prided myself on teaching them independent thinking, but they taught me about interdependence! While only first, second, and third graders, they had already accepted more responsibility and group accountability than most American high school students. Sadly, I knew *I* hadn't taught that!

My year of teaching on Yap stirred something deep within me and began to change the way I thought about the teaching process. These students introduced me to a new paradigm of classroom interaction with different expectations for relationships, both between students and their teachers and among students. Out of these experiences I developed a keen interest and commitment to research teaching and learning in differing cultural contexts. After a period of graduate study at the University of Pittsburgh, I returned to Yap in 1979 to spend a year examining in greater depth the culture of teaching and learning in Yap High School. At about the same time, Sherwood and I began serving with SIL International and other mission organizations as researchers and consultants on issues concerning cultural systems, learning styles, and cultural communication. In the years since I taught on Yap, I have taken opportunities to teach and observe in classes around the world. It has been an exciting journey: Every time I think I understand what is happening, I am surprised by something new. Perhaps one of the hallmarks of an abiding passion is that it always provokes new thinking and learning.

Cultural Context of Schooling

Looking back from this perspective in my life, the tension and frustration I experienced in my second teaching job in McKeesport, Pennsylvania, was due to my misunderstanding of the cultural context of schooling. I had grown up in a middle-class neighborhood in northeastern Philadelphia, and my schooling experience from first grade through college was predominantly in a middle-class social context. My first teaching job in Lombard, Illinois, was in a middle-class junior high school. Teaching in that context was easy for me. My cultural background and the culture of the school were a natural fit, and I was very successful in that classroom context.

Junior high school in McKeesport was a different story. While the teachers and the principal in McKeesport Junior High School had middle-class backgrounds and education, the students came from inner-city neighborhoods and welfare or working-class black or immigrant families. I failed to understand that the students brought their cultural habits and expectations with them to my classroom. These cultural differences had a dramatic effect on our interaction in a classroom context. I learned from this experience that schooling in the urban centers of the United States is a multicultural challenge. To be effective in the city, I had to learn to teach cross-culturally.

Instead of adapting my teaching to meet the students in their culture, I responded in McKeesport by trying to teach them the "proper" culture of school. This is a common practice in American schooling. I saw this most graphically when I taught in the Head Start program on the island of Yap. The primary purpose of the program was to teach Yapese children the American culture of schooling. We introduced them to classroom routines, the role of the teacher, and a particular style of teaching that uses questions and responses. We even introduced them to our culture of food. Head Start was about what Philip Jackson (1968) calls the "hidden curriculum."

My Yap elementary school experience, teaching grades 1 through 3 in a single classroom, pushed me to rethink my role and practice as a teacher. Early on I realized that I could not teach the curriculum for three grades on my own. As I interacted with the students, I discovered that they were willing partners with me. The older children were eager assistants in helping the younger children to learn. The students also helped me to understand their cultural differences and patterns of working together. I learned as much as I taught in that elementary school classroom.

Since 1977, Sherwood and I have been conducting adult workshops in Latin America, Africa, and Asia. The participants, who are missionaries and national church leaders, come from diverse cultural contexts. The lessons I learned in the Yap elementary school classroom have proven to be extremely valuable as I work in these multicultural contexts of adult learners.

Every training or educational situation has a cultural context of teaching and learning. Usually the organization that plans and funds the school or workshop establishes the context. The definition of curriculum, the scheduling of time, and the organization of learning are structured around a set of cultural expectations that belong to the sponsoring organization. While teaching from a single cultural perspective can work, teachers will be more effective if they recognize the importance of cultural context.

One of the first steps in teaching cross-culturally is to clarify and value the cultural distinctives of the participants. In our West Africa workshop on partnership, we divided the participants into two groups, missionaries and Africans. We asked each group to arrive at a definition of partnership and to write their understandings on the blackboard. From these reports, participants saw immediately how different their ideas were about partnership. Merely clarifying and valuing these differences led to much more effective learning for all participants in the workshop.

The teacher's role is to create the most appropriate context within which students can learn. As we worked with these adults, we found it important to help them focus on both their differences and their common ground of spiritual commitment for ministry. By helping them focus on their common commitments, we played the role of facilitator, creating situations in which they and we could learn together.

As you can see from these illustrations, the cultural context of schooling is important for teachers at every level of education. Whether working with elementary or secondary students in cities in the United States or in Bible schools in Africa or Latin America, teachers face many cultural issues. Students will always bring their culture to the classroom. As teachers we may be tempted to impose our culture of school on those students and push them to adhere to our hidden curriculum. Throughout the pages of this book, we will try to help you gain a deeper understanding of the complexity of the cultural beings we call students and of the diverse opportunities you have as a teacher to create a context in which they can learn and grow.

A Teacher Is a Person with Power

If you have ever failed an exam or gotten a grade lower than you thought you deserved, you understand that a teacher is a person with power. It is extremely important to recognize that a teacher has power in relation to students. This power is derived from a teacher's authority, which has two dimensions: skill authority and role authority.

Teachers have skill authority by virtue of the special education and preparation they have to serve as teachers in the classroom. Most teachers have a significantly higher level of education than their students, and most specialized in a particular subject area, making them experts in an aspect of the curriculum. In addition, over a period of years, teachers develop their professional skills through the experience of teaching and through continuing education. Teachers, therefore, bring to their classrooms a particular authority that comes from their education and skill.

Teachers also have a special authority derived from the role. A person in a teaching role controls the subject matter taught in the class, defines the schedule within which that subject matter is taught, plans the lessons for each day, and defines the evaluation framework for assessing students. A particular concern to students is the fact that teachers control the positive or negative assessment of their performance. But a teacher controls much more. A teacher can make students stand in a line, wait to go to the bathroom, or insist that they be quiet. By the time students become young or mature adults, they have so internalized these rules and regulations that they obey them without direction from the teacher. For experienced students, the controlled order of classroom behavior is automatic. Adult students bring notebooks and paper, expect exams, sit through a class regardless of whether they are suffering physiological discomfort, and often follow the directions of the teacher without question.

The power that a teacher has lies in the control a teacher exercises over things that are of value to students. Usually this control is focused on outcomes such as grades, advancement, credit toward a degree, or certification of qualification for employment. The structure of control encompasses most aspects of classroom life.

Both teachers and students bring their independent wills to the classroom. It is in the contests of will that students and teachers struggle for power in their relationships with one another. A teacher may will to affirm, rebuke, encourage, destroy, build up, or tear down students. Students may will to obey, disobey, contradict, comply, harass, or submit to the authority of the teacher. Through the engagement of will, teachers and students create an emotional climate that defines the characteristics of teacher-student relationships and student-student relationships in the classroom.

When cultural differences are added to these power issues, there is a potential for misunderstanding and conflict. As we think about teaching cross-culturally, we recognize that Christian teachers have a great responsibility as they seek to honor Christ and be filled with the Spirit in their teaching relationships. A power struggle may become a critical factor in one's effectiveness as a Christian teacher.

Culture as Palace and Prison

As I already related, my first teaching assignment was in a middle-class community where students shared with me a common cultural heritage. It was a wonderful year that affirmed my gifts as a teacher and rewarded me for my investment in the development of these young people. In that context, my culture served me well. I understood what to expect from the students, they understood what to expect from me, and our mutual relationship was rewarding and fulfilling.

My second teaching assignment was much more difficult. The students did not like me, I did not understand them, and we struggled daily with power issues in the classroom. I insisted that they conform to my schedule and respond according to my direction. They resisted, harassed me, and generally worked to make my life miserable. Neither I nor my students understood that we were prisoners of our cultures. I assumed that the only proper way to run a classroom was the way I had experienced it growing up and the way I had achieved success in my first teaching job. They in turn saw no reason to conform to my routines and patterns of relating that from their perspective were oppressive, boring, and unhelpful.

Our struggles soon became a contest of power. I sent those who refused to conform to my demands to the principal's office. On occasion the principal dismissed them from school. Others, recognizing my will and my commitment to force them to conform, submitted grudgingly to my demands and expectations. A few at times harassed me to such an extent that I went home weeping in frustration. I am sure there were times when students went home deeply frustrated and crying to their parents about their experience with me.

What was the problem? The basic argument in this book is that our culture serves us well when it is the only culture in focus. In fact, it is a palace when there are no other contesting voices around us, when we can live fairly comfortable, ordered lives in the context of our own cultural system. However, when we are pushed into relationships that are outside the boundaries of our culture, that culture becomes a prison to us. We are blind to other ways of seeing and doing things, and we assume that our way is the only way that is appropriate. We become frustrated and angry with those who insist on breaking our rules, and we attempt to enforce our rules on them. In such a context, the more powerful people are usually successful in forcing their cultural way on others and making them conform to their way of life.

In my (Sherwood's) earlier work (Lingenfelter 1998), I argued that all of us are prisoners to our culture. While our culture serves us in many useful ways, we become so enamored of it that we cannot imagine any other way of relating to people. We assume that others will do things our way, and we interpret their behavior in accord with our own values and understanding. As a consequence, we are blind to cultural differences and do not even think to question why people act or think differently than we do.

Jesus: The Master Teacher

As Christian educators, we should seek to model our work on the principles and values taught by Jesus and his apostles in the Bible. Jesus Christ is our master teacher and provides both principles and examples of effective teaching. The mystery of the incarnation, Jesus "being in very nature God" yet taking on a human body and becoming a servant to humanity (Phil. 2:6–9), provides a powerful analogy that can guide us in teaching cross-culturally.

The Gospel of Luke (2:41–52) reveals that Jesus began his young life as a learner. Luke tells how Jesus departed the company of his parents and relatives to stay in Jerusalem to learn more in the temple. His frantic parents discovered him after three days of searching "sitting among the teachers, listening to them and asking them questions" (Luke 2:46). We have reflected often on this passage, pondering the significance of this young man who was "in very nature God" sitting among the experts in his culture and learning from them.

If Jesus felt it necessary to begin his career listening and asking questions, how can we do less? We have tried to model this example in our teaching and service by spending hours in places like Yap, listening to the experts in the culture and asking them questions. We have learned that the only effective way to enter into another culture is to make its experts our teachers.

In Luke's story, Mary and Joseph "were astonished" and confused by Jesus' behavior. Luke 2:52 concludes the story by saying, "Jesus grew in wisdom and stature, and in favor with God and men." This conclusion suggests that Jesus was committed to mastering the knowledge and habits of his culture and that by doing so he grew in favor with people and with God.

The teaching phase of Jesus' life shows that he indeed mastered the cultural ways of the people around him. His lessons were filled with quotations from Scripture, stories based on local economic and social life, and parables that drew on a deep understanding of their way of life. His classroom was every-where—in a house, on a boat, on the seashore, on the plains, in the hills, or on the road. He taught lessons using the contexts of work, family, community, and religious life. Using practical demonstrations, he healed the sick, cast out demons, and addressed people in the midst of broken relationships or fam-ily crises. Jesus engaged his students during their work, on the Sabbath, and in public debate. He met them at any place where he could effectively teach them to think in new ways about their relationship with him, God, and the world.

In Philippians 2:6–7, Paul tells us that Jesus was "in very nature God" yet "made himself nothing, taking the very nature of a servant, being made in human likeness." This text suggests that Jesus was 100 percent God and 100 percent human. If we can imagine it, Jesus was a 200-percent person. Jesus was obe-dient to Mary and Joseph and to his eternal Father. He lived as a respected and honored Jewish rabbi but also as the Son of Man, sent on a mission by his eternal Father. He obeyed his Father's commands and submitted himself to the betrayal of his friends and to crucifixion by the Roman authorities.

What relevance does this have for teaching cross-culturally? As I (Sherwood) suggested in *Ministering Cross-Culturally* (1986), Jesus is the example we are to follow in our lives. Paul makes this clear in Ephesians 5:1–2: "Be imitators of God, therefore, as dearly loved children and live a life of love, just as Christ loved us and gave himself up for us as a fragrant offering and sacrifice to God."

It is obviously impossible to be born into another culture as Jesus was born into the Jewish world. Many of us enter another culture as adults and take on teaching responsibilities as an assignment for our daily work. But we, like Jesus, should begin as learners, listening and asking questions. Our responsibility is to love the people to whom we go and to give up part of our identity and values for their sake to become effective servants of Christ among them.

The Incarnational Teacher: A 150-Percent Person

In *Ministering Cross-Culturally*, I (Sherwood) suggested that those who minister cross-culturally should seek to become 150-

percent persons—75 percent birth culture and 75 percent incarnate in the culture of ministry. Judy and I were both born as middle-class Anglo-Americans. We were raised to be proud of our culture, to respect our parents, and to appreciate the way of life that we knew in the United States. We came to know Christ as young people and learned to worship in a Christian church. We earned bachelor's degrees from a Christian college and doctoral degrees from a secular university. We have had a lifetime of learning to conform to our cultural world. When we went to the island of Yap in the late 1960s, we were suddenly thrust into a situation in which we had to become less American and more Yapese.

When teaching cross-culturally, the ideal is to become less American (75 percent) and more like those we teach (at best 75 percent) and therefore 150-percent persons. Obviously we can never stop being the children of our parents and of our culture. But to be effective in a new culture, we must learn a host of new behaviors that are not part of our way of life. For example, in Yap we had to learn new values about time and to think differently about obligations of relationships. We discovered that the Yapese way of dealing with crises was far different from our way, and we had to adjust to their way.

Learning about our differences was oftentimes stressful because it usually occurred in day-to-day life rather than in a classroom. We learned by making mistakes and seeing the pain that we caused others. We learned by watching and listening and asking questions. We learned by participating with people in the daily and the crisis events of their lives. In a short period of time, we had to give up values and practices we had learned to cherish and to take on new ways of doing things that were strange for us. To succeed in a new context, we had to take on a new cultural way of life.

When I accepted the Yap elementary school teaching assignment described at the beginning of this chapter, I had already spent more than a year living among the Yapese people and learning their language. Because of this village experience, I saw the behaviors of the children differently than I would have seen them when I first arrived on Yap. I had a framework within which to interpret the responses of children, and that framework provided creative ways for bridging cultural differences and bringing these children together to learn.

Perhaps the most important thing that happened to me was coming to the realization that I could no longer rely on my past experiences and identity as a teacher in the United States. My cultural identity had changed because I had adopted many of the habits and behaviors of the Yapese villagers. These new habits and behaviors increased my repertoire of options for responding to students and helped me engage the students in different ways. I had become at least a 120-percent person, perhaps 80 percent American and 40 percent Yapese. I saw my role as a teacher as much more complex and varied than I had understood it in McKeesport. And I interpreted the students' behaviors and values from two cultural frameworks, the one I understood in America and the one I now understood in Yap. Because of these two different frames, I was able to avoid the temptation to use my power as a teacher to force students to conform to my way of doing things; instead, I began to see how best to help them grow and learn in their context.

Jesus, a person with infinite power as the only begotten Son of God, refused to use that power to achieve an end that would have benefited him. He taught his disciples that the way of the world was to lord it over others, but he was among them as a servant. At his last supper with them, he washed their feet and then challenged them to follow his example (John 13).

Throughout this book, we will reflect on the example Jesus gave us as an incarnational teacher. We will ask when it might be appropriate to give up our cultural practices, ways of doing things, or values about effectiveness. We will ask when it is appropriate to take on the structure, values, and relationship styles of the people we seek to teach and to serve. We know we cannot stop being Americans, yet we also know we can learn to be much more. To assist you in this process, we will seek to clarify and to value the cultural distinctives you will encounter as you teach cross-culturally. We will then try to highlight the issues that bring conflict into your relationships with students and colleagues. Pointing to biblical principles, revealed especially in the life and teaching ministry of Christ, we hope to show you a common spiritual ground between you and those you seek to serve. Finally, we will try to guide you to the development of strategies that will facilitate your learning and the learning of students in your classroom.

two

The Hidden Curriculum

Recently I watched a video on downhill skiing. To dramatize the fears that beginning skiers have, the video showed a baby sitting alone on the grass reading a book titled *How to Walk*. With grown-up logic, the baby then attempted to stand and move, with predictable results. I was struck by the cultural biases of the video makers, as they caricatured learning in America. The baby was on his own, sitting alone, trying to learn a complex task from a manual. Occasionally, adult hands appeared to assist the baby's attempts to walk, but the video portrayed learning to walk (which in this case was a metaphor for learning to ski) as a task in which the learner was on his own. While this was clearly an attempt at humor, the video captured a key aspect of the culture of learning in America. The burden of learning rests heavily on the individual, and while help is available, one must ask for it. Asking is humiliating, so we often go to the instructional manual first.

On Yap, children are rarely alone. They are almost always surrounded by older siblings and adults, and learning is always a corporate process. From birth onward, Yapese children are nurtured within a societal context that teaches them the value of belonging to a group and conforming to its expectations. As an outcome of that training, children learn not to question those who are older but rather to learn by observing what adults do and imitating them as much as possible. Occasionally, adults give direct instruction to children, but usually they address one or more children rather than singling out an individual.

By the time Yapese children are of school age, they have mastered a large body of knowledge about the world in which they live. I remember walking down a path with two Yapese elementary school boys at my side. Each pointed to various plants along the path and asked me to name them. I, who had grown up in a city, knew nothing about plants in my own culture. Finally, one of the boys stopped, turned to me with his hands on his hips, and said loudly, "Didn't your mother teach you *anything?*"

In contrast to Yapese adults, middle-class Anglo-American parents focus on their children individually and gauge their learning progress separately. For example, on Yap, Sherwood and I often read to our daughter Jennifer before she went to bed. During the reading time, we would ask her questions: "What color is the ball? What sound does the pig make? Where did the spider go when the rains came?" In so doing, we were teaching her to take meaning from a text and to ask questions about things she did not know. Jennifer learned early to ask questions, to make observations about the world around her, and to engage as a conversational partner with adults. For Anglo-Americans, learning the alphabet, reading, and now video and musical knowledge are more important than imitating adult routines and behaviors. Parents single out a child who is slow and often invest special effort in assisting that child to catch up to his or her peers.

The Challenge: One-Culture Thinking

George Spindler (1987) compares a number of classic case studies involving culture to illustrate how different child-rearing strategies produce the kind of adults desired in each cultural setting. In Palau, a neighboring island to Yap, children are socialized early not to make emotional attachments. Among the Hano, a North American Indian tribe, adults use ritual and ceremony to teach children, and each child is initiated into a cult at age nine. Among the Eskimo, children assume responsibilities early in life and are included in adult affairs. They learn by doing and observing, and adults constantly admonish and direct. Spindler's comparison shows that educational socialization by parents has a specific cultural agenda, just as western schooling has a cultural agenda.

As I watched my daughter become socialized into the Yapese tradition, I realized that older children were always responsible for younger ones and that children learned physical independence early. The first time I saw my two-year-old daughter with a huge machete in her hand I cringed, but because other children also wielded these sharp instruments, I tried to refrain from reacting like a hysterical American mother by grabbing it. Because knives are an essential part of Yap life, employed to cut brush, open coconuts, and even clean fingernails, parents guide children early in the proper ways to use them.

I also noticed how early children developed an identity as part of a group. Children sat with adults and listened to their talk late into the evening. Often they fell asleep wherever they happened to be, and their mothers would carry them inside, where they slept with others in the family. We had a very small plywood and tin house, with a bedroom at either end and a main room in the middle. We prided ourselves on the fact that our two-year-old, Jennifer, had her own bedroom. It soon became evident that Yapese mothers thought I was extremely cruel for forcing my child to sleep alone. After a year on Yap, Jennifer began resisting going to bed, often pleading with us to allow her to sleep with the children across the yard. She yearned to be part of a group in a way that I as an adult could only observe.

It was not until my Yap experience that I began to see how different child-rearing strategies produce different adults. My purpose in relating this is not to focus on Yapese or American practices but rather to recognize the importance of observing and participating in daily life to understand the choices people make. For example, having seen how children are trained to be physically self-sufficient and collectively interdependent, I should have been able to predict the clean-up session described earlier. However, I had not yet translated my observations into an understanding of the implications that such early training would have on the decisions made by the students in the classroom.

The pedagogical adaptations I incorporated into my classroom were the direct result of the experiences I had on Yap. If I had not learned about Yapese culture, the task of teaching on Yap would have been much more difficult. The first thing a new teacher should do, therefore, is spend time absorbing the surrounding culture. It provides clues to behaviors and values that will be reflected in the classroom. Often, however, a teacher assumes his or her duties within days of arrival into a new culture, and the opportunity to observe and learn, if it comes at all, occurs too late to be of help.

The Issue: Hidden Curriculum

The teaching year on Yap expanded my understanding of teaching and learning. While I was simply bewildered at the cultural differences evident in the McKeesport context, my experience on Yap enabled me to grasp what Philip Jackson (1968) calls the "hidden curriculum." Jackson noted that schooling always occurs in a larger cultural context, and the "hidden curriculum" is the cultural agenda for learning that surrounds schooling.

If we think about education as the entire process of cultural transmission (Spindler 1987), schooling with its formal curriculum is a very small part (see fig. 2.1). While as educators we focus most of our efforts on schooling, the larger circle surrounding it actually carries the weight of learning. The hidden curriculum is the cultural learning that surrounds the much smaller "stated curriculum" of schooling. This hidden curriculum is "caught" rather than "taught."

In recent research on the cultural learning that surrounds a stated curriculum, certain themes surfaced regularly, particularly ones of equity. Teachers called on boys more than on girls. Students in a dorm ignored an Asian student because her accent was difficult to understand. Teachers called on blue-eyed students more often than on brown-eyed students. In my preparation as an educator, my teachers trained me to deal with the small circle of stated curriculum but did not even consider the

Figure 2.1

Education as Cultural Transmission

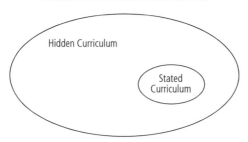

wider circle of cultural transmission. As I found out first in Mc-Keesport and then on Yap, learning about the hidden curriculum is essential in order to teach the stated curriculum effectively. The hidden curriculum represents the cultural values transmitted in the schooling process. Without understanding these, an educator does a poor job of teaching the stated curriculum.

The Logic: Applying Other-Culture Perspectives

To be an effective teacher cross-culturally, one must learn how to apply the insights gained from cultural observation to practical issues in the classroom. Gregory Bateson (1972), in a provocative article on logic and communication, established a framework for discussing the learning process that explains some of the struggles involved in grasping the cultural issues of teaching and learning.

Bateson recognized that all learning contains components of trial and error. After examining the types of errors people make and the steps they take to correct the errors, he marked three points on a continuum of the learning process: zero, level-1, and level-2 learning (see table 2.1). In zero learning, there are no trial and error corrections. For example, many years ago, a friend invited me to her house at night. She had given me explicit directions on how to get there, and I followed them carefully. However, I could not find her house. I could get to her neighborhood but not to her house. I went back to the beginning of the last part of the directions and retraced my steps. Still I could not

Table 2.1

Levels of Learning

Learning Levels	Trial and Error Corrections	Behavioral Changes
Zero	None	None
Level 1	In-context corrections	Existing alternatives Improved performance
Level 2	New context alternatives New context corrections	New and old alternatives New performance New context effectiveness

(Based on Bateson 1972, 279–308)

find it. Four times I retraced my steps. Finally, on the fifth try, I decided to turn in the opposite direction. Sure enough, I found her house very quickly. Those early attempts were examples of zero learning. I did not engage in trial and error but followed the same scenario each time. It was not until the fifth time, when I tried the direction opposite from the one I had written down (since it was obviously not working), that I actually engaged in level-1 learning.

Bateson suggests that most of us in our daily living engage in level-1 learning, trial and error with minor in-context corrections. We learn how to drive a car or identify psychological learning theories with varying degrees of ease. My undergraduate education training was such; I was told how to establish discipline, present material, and motivate my students within the context of white, middle-class families and schools. When my McKeesport students did not respond as they were "supposed" to, I was lost.

Level-2 learning requires the identification of a new set of alternatives from which a choice is made. Lulled into complacency by the erroneous belief that all children respond alike, I tried to apply principles from my suburban junior high experiences to the inner-city youth of McKeesport. According to Bateson's analysis, I did not learn the inner-city youth context but rather tried alternatives from my earlier experiences as a middle-class student and teacher. I applied level-1 solutions to a level-2 problem. On Yap, I began to observe new alternatives in the Yap culture. I saw that my students were independent physically; they did not come to school to be baby-sat, and they were used to taking charge and doing whatever tasks had to be accomplished. They also functioned as a group. I began to apply this knowledge to classroom strategy, and the results were far better than in McKeesport! I drew new alternatives from my students' context and experimented with new choices for teaching, which improved my performance. By encouraging culturally appropriate group learning exercises, I saw students thrive in their learning environment.

Yet I was not always successful in this endeavor; sometimes I relied on old alternatives rather than continuing to learn from the context. An example of my failure on Yap to decipher the hidden curriculum occurred when teaching the color wheel during a Head Start class. The first day I confidently held it up and had the students repeat the colors in English after me. They did fine until they came to the colors blue and green. I patiently went over these colors again and again until they could repeat verbatim what I had said. Only ten years later in graduate school, when reading about differences in cultural perceptions of color, did I realize what I had done. In my frustration, I had failed to ask *why* my young students knew all the colors except blue and green. I now understand that on this tiny island surrounded by the Pacific Ocean, they use many words to capture the distinctions of blue and green necessary to function effectively in their environment. I had solved the color wheel ambiguity by forcing a level-1 solution on a level-2 problem.

To be an effective cross-cultural teacher, one must learn the other-culture perspective and derive from it new alternatives for the challenges faced in a classroom. Relying on past experience will often lead to misunderstanding and failure. Only by understanding the other-culture context can we identify appropriate alternatives for teaching that will have maximum effectiveness for student learning.

Hidden Curriculum as Cultural Bias

My (Sherwood's) role in this book is to bring biblical perspectives to the challenges that Christian teachers face as they seek to increase their effectiveness in teaching cross-culturally.

After more than thirty years of researching and consulting on these issues, I have concluded that all people hold cultural values and systems of relating that, on the one hand, serve them quite effectively at home but, on the other hand, blind them to the values and systems of others. Anthropologist Mary Douglas (1982) uses the term "cultural bias" to describe this blinding and confining effect of culture.

In my earlier work (Lingenfelter 1996, 1998), I suggested that the Bible speaks clearly about this human condition in culture. The apostle Peter writes, "You were redeemed from the empty way of life handed down to you from your forefathers . . . with the precious blood of Christ" (1 Peter 1:18–19). In the Book of Romans, Paul writes, "God has imprisoned all human beings in their own disobedience only to show mercy to them all" (Rom. 11:32 NJB). We see our cultural bias as part of the "prison of disobedience," and we look to Scripture to lead us to freedom. The Gospels depict Jesus challenging the cultural assumptions of his day. The Sermon on the Mount rejects the widely held assumption that the prosperous and powerful in Jewish society are the righteous. Jesus rejects Jewish customs surrounding the Sabbath and overturns many of the cultural assumptions about the law and godliness. In a similar way, we need to question our cultural assumptions and values.

Every teacher has been nurtured in a specific culture and has a specific cultural bias about teaching and learning. This cultural bias is useful and effective in the setting that nurtured it, but as "hidden curriculum" it creates blindness, error, and conflict when used in a different culture. Further, teachers and students are "prisoners" of their cultures and habits. Unaware of their hidden curriculum, they find change extremely difficult apart from the empowering grace of God through Jesus Christ. While as Christian teachers we depend on God's grace, we have the responsibility to step out in faith and to engage in the disciplines of loving and learning to become effective cross-cultural teachers.

The illustrations above showed how level-1 teaching and learning engage the patterns and practices familiar to us; we teach and learn in the context of our cultural bias. To achieve level-2 teaching and learning, we must recognize our cultural bias as a prison and look beyond it to discover new values, processes, and contexts. We must be open to different ways of thinking and learning and be willing to adopt new ways of looking at the learner, the classroom, and our practices of teaching. We must recognize that the curriculum we teach is only a small part of what students will and must learn and that their success with the curriculum will depend on how well we master the hidden curriculum.

To begin the journey toward becoming 150-percent persons, we must add to our cultural repertoire. The first principle is to become a learner in the new cultural context. Several outlines for observing the context of schooling already exist, notably the one developed by Jules Henry (1976) that follows the procedure begun by George Peter Murdock in his *Outline of Cultural Materials* (1987). However, each chapter that follows contains questions that will help teachers learn about new cultural contexts of teaching and learning. These questions focus on more than just schooling, because in thinking about education as the transmission of culture, one needs to examine the larger circle of the hidden curriculum.

Even more importantly, we must begin to think about our faith in Jesus Christ as the beginning of our liberation from the prison of disobedience and from our cultural bias. Jesus sets forth the principles essential to learning and living outside our culture, yet we apply them as if they were level-1 solutions to problems. The challenge is to learn about the new context, then to apply biblical principles for working within that context. As Paul reminds us in Philippians 2:1–5, we are to regard others as better than ourselves, make their interests at least equal to our own, and have the attitude of Jesus as we seek to serve others. The practical application of this passage is to see each challenge as a level-2 problem. Teaching cross-culturally requires that we learn to think outside our cultural and contextual expectations and to look for solutions beyond our training, experience, and expertise.

Research/Reflection Questions

1. Think about your schooling experience, and try to bring to mind at least two learning crises that impacted you (e.g., being required to dance in physical education class when

your church forbade dancing). What was significant in each case? What hidden curriculum values can you identify from these experiences?

2. Visit an elementary classroom for approximately two hours and take notes on what you observe. How does the teacher relate to the students? How are students punished? rewarded? How do the students interact with one another? Do they work independently or interdependently? What cultural values are apparent based on your observations?

three

Understanding Traditional Learning Strategies

At the Yap high school, I watched some Yapese boys learning from an American teacher how to take apart a Volkswagen engine. This teacher had been there long enough to understand that Yapese boys learn best by watching. Patiently, he took apart the engine, put it back together, took it apart again, and then put it back together. Only a few students asked questions. Then he encouraged the students to do it. He walked away and let them work in groups of two and three. Very slowly they began to duplicate the task, taking out the parts of the engine, laying them out, and putting them back together again. Not all the students felt competent at first, so they continued to watch until they were ready to try it themselves.

Earlier I described how in teaching African American seventh graders in Pennsylvania I misjudged the need to understand their learning strategies. When I arrived on Yap, I knew I would encounter an exotic culture, and I expected to spend time learning it in order to understand what was happening. For over a year I sat on my front porch, engaging in conversation with my neighbors and their children. I watched mothers teach their young children to observe rather than to ask questions of their elders. I watched children learn by imitating their mothers as the mothers swept the yard, built a fire, cut coconuts, and peeled yams or taro for cooking. I observed the patterns of women working in gardens with their children around them. The women worked for a time together, then sat and talked together while nursing babies, alternating work and extended periods of conversation throughout the day. When I observed the Yap high school class ten years later, I understood where and how the students had learned to learn.

Stephen Harris (1984) helps us better understand these indigenous learning patterns through a case study of Australian aborigines. This study was undertaken in an effort to explore the discontinuities between the culture of a traditional community and the culture of school. For our purposes, a traditional community is one in which the adults have little or no experience with formal education and in which most of the members participate in a subsistence or peasant farming way of life. Modern schools are associated with industrial economies that require most people to have formal education to participate in the workforce. These two settings represent vastly different social learning contexts, yet each offers insights into frustrations that western-trained educators experience in non-western schools. They also stimulate new thinking about how to communicate in the classroom.

Observation and Imitation

Learning by observation and imitation are strategies found around the world. Harris notes that a large gap often exists between the time when the observation begins and when the skill is exercised. A person may watch a skill for weeks before attempting it. The observation process usually takes place without questions being asked. In some cases, this is because people place substantial taboos on the use of questions. When a young Yapese man took our son Joel fishing, he was astounded at Joel's questions. He gently rebuked Joel, and when they returned, he said he had never heard a boy ask so many questions. On Yap, a child or youth usually does not ask older people questions; instead, they hone their skills of observation.

Visual learning is a culturally appropriate way to learn. People simply observe. The students watched how the instructor dismantled the engine. It was done in a particular order. They assumed it must be done that way. When one is dependent on memory, one often uses rehearsal strategies, going through the steps over and over. The order in which something is done is helpful to remembering.

Harris makes a distinction between learning by observation and learning by imitation. Observation may take place over a long period of time, whereas with imitation the task is immediately applied. Harris says that one imitates a person whom one admires. This was certainly true in a particular Yapese shop class. I chose to observe the class because students told me they admired the patience of their American teacher.

Harris suggests that aborigines prefer observation and imitation, perhaps because these methods have proven effective in their harsh natural environment. Because so little in their environment changes over long periods of time, children can learn the needed skills by participation. The traditional knowledge is reliable and effective, providing all the parents and the children need to know for a satisfying life.

Learning by Doing—Trial and Error

Learning by doing is an efficient way of learning something. For some skills it may be the only effective way. Verbal explanation of a learning procedure is difficult for people who have learned through nonverbal means. For example, Yapese young people love to play card games. However, I could never figure out the rules because none of them could explain what they were doing. They had learned the games by observing and by making mistakes and being corrected. They kept saying to me, "You just have to play it, and we will tell you whether you are right or wrong."

Aborigines learn through real-life activities rather than by practicing in contrived settings. The activities are ends in themselves and not means to a future end. A colleague of mine who teaches in Africa tells of trying to teach basketball to his students. He could never get them to run drills. He would explain the importance of drilling, how if they learned to drill they would learn to dribble and to shoot baskets, which would help them play the game better. His students refused. They kept telling him that drilling was not basketball. The only way they could really learn to play basketball was by playing the game. They had to learn in the activity rather than in a contrived setting.

People who learn best in real-life situations find it difficult to transfer the processes from one context to another. A friend in Brazil tells of trying to teach addition to adult tribal Indians. The written numbers did not mean anything until she used turtles in two basins and moved them back and forth according to the equations she was trying to teach. Using any object such as blocks or balls would not have sufficed. These men needed to connect the abstract numbers to something concrete in their world. People who see each activity as an end in itself miss the logical possibility of connecting principles. Each learning task has its own practical end, and these learners have difficulty transferring principles to other settings. Yapese and aboriginal school children do not understand the need or importance of transferring principles from one context to another.

Rote Learning and Traditional Knowledge

According to Harris, aborigines use rote learning primarily for learning proverbs, songs, and stories. Aboriginal society has a concrete body of knowledge rather than a theoretical body of knowledge. Man's spiritual nature, the meaning of existence, the best political system, or even women's rights are not philosophical or moral questions open for discussion. Rather, they are the concrete givens of existence, established by stories of creation. The stories are passed on for the concrete knowledge they contain and the pleasure they give, thus making verbal instruction about their content redundant. On Yap, people told me that stories told orally are more accurate than those written down because a written story represents only one person's opinion, whereas an oral story is subject to the collective corrections of its hearers.

Aboriginal society is also parochial in its attitude and outlook. Traditionally, aborigines were not conscious of a need to know what was happening in Russia, or in America, or even among other aboriginal tribes. Each local community was the most important, and things that happened in the world had to be related to it to have any meaning. As a consequence, when teaching such people, it is difficult to introduce concepts that are abstract or that originate from a place outside their understanding. Harris writes that the aboriginal people live in an eternal present where the future is not a serious issue. Even the past is not a topic that must be talked out in order for accuracy to be established (Harris 1984, 80–81).

Finally, he says that these people do not have a felt need to have all their questions answered. That need would necessarily involve verbal discussion. However, even in traditional settings, verbal instruction must be employed occasionally. For example, if a task has a ritual significance or it seems too difficult to learn by trial and error, people verbalize the instructions. They may also verbalize them in ritual and stories about the group's history. Harris mentions that this keen observation style makes learning through film and pictures a useful approach. A film can be rewound and shown over and over, allowing for the same kind of visual learning strategies with which they are familiar (Harris 1984, 83).

Traditional Learning and Incarnational Teaching

Modern educators have commonly rejected imitation and rote learning techniques. They have argued that these strategies limit creativity and innovation in learning. Yet Scripture teaches us that these techniques have been employed for thousands of years to enrich one's life in community and walk with God. In the Book of Job, one of Job's friends reminds him that "those who came before us will teach you. They will teach you from the wisdom of former generations" (8:10 NLT). The Psalms and Proverbs repeatedly proclaim the value of memorizing Scripture and meditation (repetition of the words) for learning to live a meaningful social, moral, and spiritual life. We propose that good teaching in any culture will include traditional learning techniques and that a teacher who wants to be a Christlike servant in a cross-cultural setting will try to make learning as context specific and real to life as possible. To achieve this we must include learning by observation and imitation, learning by trial and error, learning through real-life activities, and learning in context-specific settings.

Some experienced teachers will object, believing that observation and imitation lead to memorization without understanding. Students who want to imitate their teachers copy down notes verbatim and memorize texts so they will get it "right." Western teachers complain that students memorize information voraciously but almost never seem to understand it. They despair that students may never reach the "Aha" principle, the understanding that follows rote memorizing. In my own undergraduate training, I was taught that rote learning is not real learning.

Several years ago a young Russian couple lived with us for a year. The wife was an astute observer and imitator and progressed rapidly in learning English. One night as we sat around the dinner table, she suddenly exclaimed, "Now I understand!" When we asked her to explain, she related an English dialogue about a family at supper that she had memorized at age ten. Now, twelve years later, she understood what she had learned by rote so long ago. One hopes that the gap between rote memorizing and understanding does not take that long, especially if the repetition and rote learning are done in a meaningful, observable context that is complemented and supported by observation and imitation!

We do not want to wait twelve years, as the young Russian woman did, for our students to understand what we are teaching. The understanding component is very important. As the illustration shows, understanding occurs when a student suddenly finds memorized data relevant in a living context. This is exactly why we are told repeatedly in Scripture to memorize, hide the words in our heart, and meditate on them. When we unexpectedly find ourselves in a context that tests our character, we will know how to respond.

Repetitive memorization remains a much maligned skill that an incarnational teacher must reconsider. We fail our students when we take away the only verbal strategy in which they excel and replace it with several new kinds of verbal learning that are difficult for them at best. Students who are suddenly thrust into a school setting that is unfamiliar want to succeed in order to please the teacher. The best way for them to do so is by memorizing, exercising their already developed mental skill. When they can recite information back to the teacher, they expect the teacher will be happy because they have learned. When people place high value on belonging to a group, children prefer group recitation, which covers individual error and affirms collective achievement. Authority, the status of the teacher, and parental expectations all make rote learning a preferred model. A student does not have to question the teacher and will do well if he or she memorizes everything carefully. Language confusion can also be minimized using this method. When students are working in a second or third language, memorizing may be the easiest way to handle unfamiliar material.

A teacher who seeks to work within the cultural context of his or her students must also employ real-life and learning-in-context activities. School curricula often demand that students focus on learning for future reward, not necessarily present ones. As a consequence, school learning is "practice" for real life but not the same as real life. However, a learner in a traditional community context learns by doing or observing real life. In a class that uses only "out of context" instruction, students from traditional societies may fail to transfer the principles and skills learned in the school context to real life. One solution to this problem is to employ repetition, teaching the same content in as many different contexts as possible inside and outside the classroom until the process or the principle is internalized by the students. In the 1988 film *Stand and Deliver,* the Bolivian-trained teacher of an algebra class of Hispanic students in Los Angeles used this technique successfully. He made his students chant algebraic rules (e.g., "a negative times a negative equals a positive"). While most educators would not see this technique as true learning, its success in this particular classroom was no fluke. The teacher recognized that some rules just have to be learned, and learning them out loud as a group worked better than learning them individually and quietly.

Students from traditional societies often do not see the need to learn information for its own sake. They wonder why they need to study parts of speech or read from primers that do not seem to make sense. Some have never had a formal teacher, and verbal instruction is limited; teaching was never the focus of activity. When these students enter school, they suddenly face teachers who expect them to learn information that is important to others but not visibly so to them.

Master/Disciple Relationships

Harris reminds us that in some societies the only people who can teach are those with whom people have a personal, mentor-like relationship. This is precisely what the Gospels describe as "being a disciple," learning by following the master teacher. The same model is described in 1 Kings 19:19–21 and 2 Kings 2, when Elijah calls Elisha to be his student. In the Gospel of John, Jesus notes that his mentor relationship is a hierarchical one: "You call me 'Teacher' and 'Lord,' and you are right, because it is true" (13:13 NLT).

Christian teachers must build relationships with students before they can teach effectively. Among a great many tribes in Africa, a wealth-in-people concept rather than a wealth-in-information concept predominates. The teacher is seen as someone who comes alongside students to help in their struggle to learn, which involves cooperative, not individual, effort. If one does not build personal relationships with students, they cannot learn well.

Some western teachers embrace the idea of building relationships but mistakenly conclude that the appropriate way of relating is as a peer or a friend. Traditional learning often follows the hierarchy of older to younger, master to apprentice. Western educators have often ignored this principle with disastrous results. Teachers who have tried to be friends have lost respect and the right to teach. In another scenario, mission leaders, assuming local people already have relationships, have assigned the best-trained indigenous young people to teach in a church or community and have been surprised when people refused to accept them because of their youth.

A master teacher role connotes seniority, authority, and power in the context of a caring, reciprocal personal relationship. Teachers give knowledge, wisdom, and protection; students reciprocate with deference, respect, and obedience. In most traditional societies, students expect such a relationship with their teachers. Westerners who step into such roles often do not understand the expectations of their students and when under stress revert to practices they used in their home setting.

Several years ago we participated in a pre-field orientation program for a group of missionaries going to work in Micronesia. One young teacher who had strong theological training had agreed to teach in a Bible college on the island of Chuuk. The Chuukese principal had come to the training center to meet with the teacher. As they spent time together, it seemed as though they were building a positive relationship. They went to the airport together to arrange for the teacher's ticket to Micronesia. Upon their return, the Chuukese principal went immediately to the training director and said, "I do not want this man in Micronesia." The director was aghast because the mission staff felt he was well qualified for the job. He asked the man why he had changed his mind. The Micronesian replied, "Because I watched him lose his temper. I watched him get angry with the airline officials because they weren't able to take care of his situation very quickly. We are just not interested in having this kind of a person on our island." A master teacher in Chuuk is highly respected by students, but in return the teacher must demonstrate great patience and show care and compassion for them.

A western teacher can learn much from the example of Jesus in just such a setting. Throughout the Gospels, Jesus is portrayed as a master, teaching with authority and power. Yet he never exerts his power or authority against his students or the poor and helpless in the towns in which he taught. He reserves his anger for the self-righteous, powerful rulers and exercises his authority to teach, forgive sins, heal the sick, and challenge evil. In John 13, Jesus acknowledges his role as teacher and Lord over his disciples, yet he takes a towel and washes their feet. This powerful symbolic act of service captures the essence of a Christ-centered master-disciple relationship.

Research/Reflection Questions

1. Observe students playing a game. Ask them to teach you how to play it. How do their teaching methods compare to yours? Was it easy or difficult for you to learn the rules?
2. Watch how your students teach one another a new skill. Is there a great deal of verbal instruction? If not, how does one learn from the other?

four

Formal Schooling and Traditional Learning

In the Philippines in 1996, I watched a New Zealand mission-ary training a Filipina named Lucia to teach adult literacy. The missionary had prepared an excellent teacher training manual and went over it with Lucia, explaining carefully how to teach the material. When we went to the school to observe, however, we discovered that Lucia was not using the material from the text; she was teaching using rote learning strategies. The next morning the missionary teacher invited Lucia to her house and demonstrated a literacy lesson. She had Lucia practice it right there. Later we went back to the school and watched Lucia do an excellent job of presenting the material she had practiced that morning.

The moral of this story is that non-western learners do what they have learned by doing! Western teachers often prefer a step-by-step explanation of a process, a guidebook. Lucia had been told how to teach by her trainer, but she did not apply it to her own teaching. Once Lucia had observed a demonstration and had replicated it in a practice session, she then had the confidence to try the techniques that had been explained to her.

Learning by Explanation or by Doing?

When western educators train teachers, they use elaborate teacher training manuals and concentrate on developing appropriate curricula. Their objective is to describe and explain everything a teacher needs to know to teach. Teachers then teach others as they were taught. Yet teacher trainees in developing countries usually do not understand our teacher training manuals; instead, they prefer to watch us teach and then imitate us. Only after they watch and experience our unfamiliar perspectives are they able to put them into practice.

In another context in the Philippines, I listened to a Filipina literacy specialist explain that when teaching literacy training courses, she always assumes that her students will have to take the course at least four times before they are ready to teach. The better students can teach after the third time, but most students feel far more confident if they sit through it four or more times.

This trainer's insight into the importance of repetition for her students' mastery of content and skill for teaching has profound implications for western teachers in non-western contexts. Often missionaries who are training leaders assume that once a student has taken a course, he or she will be ready to assume leadership. Yet the first time through a series of courses may serve principally to acquaint the student with the teacher's style, the context of the school, and the testing process. The next time through the same courses, the student can better concentrate on observing the teacher in action and absorbing some of the content. A third time through would most likely cement the new knowledge firmly in place, especially if the observation is followed by imitation, either inside or outside the classroom. A western educator finds this approach difficult, feeling that he or she must teach a specific sequence of courses during a pre-specified period of time and that repeating a course is a waste of time. As a colleague in Papua New Guinea said, "Why are you westerners always in such a hurry? We're not!"

A second insight from this Filipina trainer is that the connection between knowing a subject and putting that knowledge into practice proceeds slowly among students. We may look at non-western students and wonder why they are so slow at learning what we teach. Yet I see the same thing at the university where I teach, both among the students and the faculty. So often I hear a student say something that indicates that the knowledge I labored to pour into him did not result in any change in his thinking. At this point I want to adopt the same exasperated posture as my young Yapese friend did so many years ago and ask him, "Didn't I teach you *anything?*" Further, I look back on my own teaching experience and cringe. Did I really think or say those things? How stupid or naive I was! Both teaching and learning are slow processes, the former because we strive to make the content clear, and the latter because each student brings a different set of experiences, learning style, and general intelligence to the classroom.

The values we hold that lead us to produce teaching manuals, to reject repetition in class, and to expect students to understand what we teach the first time we teach it are an expression of the broader culture of schooling of which we are a part. Some people have naively suggested that we should simply change schools to conform to the patterns of their students. For my doctoral dissertation (J. E. Lingenfelter 1981), I conducted an ethnographic study of Yap High School. American educators started the school in the 1960s, and by 1980, the Yapese teachers and students had changed many of the western ideas to better reflect their cultural patterns. The astounding thing was their dissatisfaction with what they had created. For many Yapese, high school was no longer school; it was too easy, and parents and students alike spoke of it with disdain. Schooling has a distinctive culture, and when elements of that culture are lost, people no longer value the experience.

Unless one is working in a very remote area, students will already have stereotypes about what school is and what it is not. School is not music and dance. School is not proverbs and folktales, and it is not where one learns indigenous knowledge. School is not amusing conversation. School has a few ceremonies and rites in it such as graduation, but very few. School is lecture, not dialogue, and it is individual oriented. When traditional learning techniques are introduced into schooling, many people will resist them because "that's not school." So in such a situation a western teacher has a double problem. She has western methods that do not work, and therefore, she wants to try indigenous methods. But the people won't let her because they want western schooling.

Learning by Questioning

As already stated, many traditional learning strategies do not emphasize asking questions. Yet western teachers spend much of their time in the classroom asking questions. What is the culture of questioning that these teachers bring to the classroom? How does this culture affect non-western or traditional learners?

In today's world, linked by radio, TV, and computer, aboriginal students can watch demonstrators on TV questioning the necessity for military intervention in Iraq and hear commentators asking questions of people concerning the collapse of the World Trade Center towers. These globalizing forces increase their need to understand the role and purpose of questions in the educational process. However, the challenge to western educators is to broaden the kinds of questions welcomed in the classroom. Often we are only interested in a certain kind of question, or else we ask an abstract question that confounds students who are trying to find the "right" answer. In other words, the kinds of questions stressed in western schools are not the kinds of questions used in traditional settings.

Shirley Brice Heath (1982) argues that the culture of questioning in most U.S. classrooms comes from the experience of middle-class families. For five years she studied three groups of students in the southern United States, a middle-class Anglo group that she called Maintown, a working-class group named Roadville, and a lower-class African American group identified as Trackton. A key discovery Heath made was that Maintown parents read bedtime stories to their children, whereas Trackton parents did not. Maintown parents not only read to their children but also engaged them as conversational partners by asking questions as they read. For example, when reading to a one-year-old, a mother might ask, "What does the doggy say?" She then expects her child to make the appropriate response. As the child matures, the questions become more sophisticated (e.g., "After the storm was over, what do you think happened to the water that overflowed the banks?"). Heath concluded that from an early age children learn to take meaning from books if they have been read to; if they have not, then the idea of answering abstract questions, especially those to which the adult already knows the answer, seems foreign.

While Maintown mothers used questions in roughly 50 percent of their interactions with their children from birth onward, the same was not true for Trackton children. These children may have been present when adults were talking, but they were not included in conversations because they were not seen as legitimate conversational partners. This difference in early socialization patterns had clear results: Anglo children went to school ready to answer questions posed by the teacher, while African American children were unprepared to cope with questions that seemed strange to them. They did not understand why a teacher would ask, "What color is the truck?" when he or she already knew the answer. These students would not answer, causing the teacher to draw the false conclusion that they did not know the answer.

Heath's research illustrates one of the many reasons why lower-class African American students have difficulty in middle-class Anglo schools in the United States. But her work offers wider implications for the study of teaching and learning cross-culturally. Both Heath and Stephen Harris (1984) have shown that children learn differently in different cultural settings and that western schooling is rooted in the middle-class culture that sustains it. Heath has demonstrated how a strong pedagogical bent toward the use of questions and verbal recitation flows from American middle-class child rearing.

Questions asked by older students in U.S. classrooms follow the same pattern as that described by Heath in elementary schools. But these students usually ask additional types of questions. The anxious student who is frantically taking notes on all the teacher says will often ask confirmation questions such as "Are you saying that global learning is the same as holistic learning?" He or she often challenges or disagrees with the teacher as well: "Are you suggesting that the ends justify the means? How can that possibly be true?" Another type of question used frequently in an American classroom digresses from the subject. A student may interrupt a professor's lecture to ask when the final exam will be.

A final type of question observed in American classrooms is the abstract question. This may be used by a bright student who is truly trying to understand or extend a concept by taking it to a new level of abstraction. Unfortunately, these types of questions often lead to exclusive discussions between the professor and the student, while others in the class feel increasingly bewildered by a conversation they do not understand. These types of questions—confirmation, digression, and abstract—illustrate the wide range of questions used in western classrooms (Portin 1993).

Framing Culturally Appropriate Questions

Educators trained in the western tradition need to recognize the cultural patterns of this style of teaching. The western tradition emphasizes the individual and achieved status. We are taught to challenge rather than to accept passively what another says, and we like to boast about how this ability to question the status quo contributes to our worldwide dominance in discovering innovative solutions to existing problems. While others may think us rude and pushy, we feel justified in questioning ideas, directives, and the like on the grounds that we are seeking to do a job better. When we teach Chinese students to raise questions and they do so in their interactions with older people in village settings, the results can be disastrous.

How can western teachers teach the culture of questioning to non-western learners? First, they must take into consideration the values of the wider society from which the students come. Cultural differences that govern the use or nonuse of questions are related to the following:

Age. In societies in which distinctions between elders and youth are particularly strong, children are taught not to ask questions of older people. They can ask questions only of peers and those younger or of lower status.

Disrespect. It would be extremely disrespectful for an Asian student to challenge the authority of the teacher.

Taboos. On Yap, one of the most surprising taboos is the one against asking a child his or her father's name. We have similar taboos in American culture, such as asking a woman how old she is.

Threat. Asking a question directly may be seen as an assault on one's prestige or status or as a challenge to displace that person. In a heated student meeting a few years ago, one student turned to another and said, "Who made you the boss over us?"

Personal. The definition of personal questions varies greatly from culture to culture. For example, when I was visiting Seoul, Korea, people repeatedly asked me how old I was. Americans do not ask a stranger that question. My husband often asks me what I'm thinking, particularly when we are engaged in a discussion and he wants to know my opinion. In some contexts, such a question would be considered intensely private, and the person would be insulted.

Material vs. moral questions. Asian children are taught to look for the moral character of a person or an action, not the material attribute, as is done in western schooling. Therefore, a question such as "How was the king dressed?" would be considered insignificant, whereas "Do you think he is lying?" would be considered entirely appropriate.

These examples by no means constitute an exhaustive catalog of cultural differences. Yet even these few should give an educator pause for reflection because they represent a different set of pedagogical rules that govern interactions. All questions are not created equal, even though in western classrooms we say that the only stupid question is the unasked one.

Bridging Cultures in Formal Schooling

The culture of formal schooling often creates a significant barrier to learning for many students. Teachers and students alike are prisoners of their cultural backgrounds. Non-western students cling to visual and rote memorization strategies learned in childhood that contribute little to success in a western-oriented classroom. Western teachers employ questioning strategies that confuse and distress students who do not understand why teachers ask culturally inappropriate questions. Yet unless the essentials of formal schooling are retained, people may not value the experience. How then do we bridge these cultural differences and create classrooms in which effective teaching and learning take place among people from different cultures?

The teacher, who has the authority to define the classroom experience, must take responsibility for creating a context that bridges cultural differences. To accomplish this the teacher must resist using power and begin as a learner. Heath (1982) has demonstrated that one needs to learn the ways people socialize their young to help these same young people succeed in a western schooling environment. To do so, a teacher should spend time outside class observing children and adults learning in the contexts of their homes and communities. The teacher will observe the ways in which children routinely learn from adults, or adults learn from one another, and should try to adapt these techniques to frame learning activities at school. The goal is not to replicate the home or community learning context but rather to help students begin learning through familiar and nonthreatening situations. By reflecting on the learning practices used in the family, the teacher will also be able to ascertain which of the typical teaching practices are *not* used by parents. He or she will know to use special care when introducing and explaining the meaning and purpose of what to him or her are familiar techniques.

The goal of the incarnational teacher is to create a learning context that is familiar to students yet stretches them beyond their previous experiences. A teacher leads students to understand the place and purpose of traditional and formal learning and helps students understand and use both. While schooling does not depend on the questioning technique, it does represent a verbal strategy that most students will encounter as they engage in the expanding global economy and technology.

Jesus was a master teacher in a traditional learning context. Jewish education emphasized memorization of the Torah and the prophets. The Pharisee sect required its members to memorize and practice an additional legal code that governed hundreds of details in daily life. Jesus began with the traditions of his people yet pushed them to think beyond the customs and boundaries of their knowledge and practices. By observing some of the techniques Jesus used, we can learn to teach in a traditional context while stretching students to think and learn outside the boundaries of that context.

One of the most common techniques employed by Jesus was the rhetorical question. The Gospel of Luke reports Jesus using rhetorical questions more than twenty times in his public teaching (e.g., 5:22–24; 6:3–5, 9–10; etc.). A teacher may begin with rhetorical questions to teach students how to think in response to queries. These questions become part of the lesson, and while people can ponder them, they are not compelled to provide a "right" answer to satisfy the teacher. Students can become comfortable with the use of questions and not worry about having to produce the correct responses. As Jesus did in his teaching, a teacher may pose a rhetorical question and wait for students to consider it before developing the thought in a new way for them.

The most common technique Jesus used in teaching was the story, and on a few occasions he asked his listeners a question at the end of the story. One of the most well-known stories is that of the Samaritan who was a good neighbor (Luke 10:25–37). In the story, three men, a priest, a Levite, and a Samaritan, pass a man, wounded, robbed, and lying on the side of the road. Jesus asks his listeners, "Which of these three was a neighbor to the man?" On another occasion Jesus asks, "Tell me, John's baptism—was it from heaven, or from men?" (Luke 20:3). In both of these situations, Jesus challenged the traditional views of his listeners by asking a question that forced them to evaluate alternative moral behaviors or interpretations of behavior.

A colleague working in Mexico City among adults developed a variation of this questioning strategy that greatly aided his students' ability to learn by defusing their anxiety. They were allowed to choose answers to written questions about a particular biblical passage, but he stressed that all the answers were correct. He wanted them to choose the one that seemed best to them and to justify their choice. The adults responded quickly to this exercise and with more thoughtful insights than when he used traditional exam questions.

After Jesus had developed intimate relationships with his disciples, he asked more difficult and probing questions. On one occasion when he was alone with his disciples, he asked, "Who do the crowds say I am?" After the disciples reported the views of the crowds, he asked, "But what about you? . . . Who do you say I am?" Peter, perhaps speaking for the group, replied, "The Christ of God" (Luke 9:18–20). The kind of question one asks plays a key role in the development of the learner.

Questions that allow the learner to reflect in a holistic way on a picture or a story may help him or her gain confidence in answering, again because the questions do not imply a right answer. Consider the following example.

> Teacher (showing a picture of people praying in a prostrate position): What's going on here? Have you ever prayed in this position?

The first question seeks a report; the second draws the students and their experiences into the response. They are not threatening questions because they simply ask for the students' interpretations. The second follow-up question helps the students voice their opinions in a safe environment and begin to answer higher level types of questions.

Sometimes questions of importance must be asked indirectly, especially if they involve ethics or emotions. Jesus confronts Simon the Pharisee, who was critical of a sinful woman who washed Jesus' feet with her tears, by telling him a story about two men who owed money to a money lender and were forgiven their debts (Luke 7:36–50). He asks Simon, "Now which of them will love him more?" (v. 42). Simon replied, "I suppose the one who had the bigger debt canceled" (v. 43). Jesus then used Simon's answer to challenge his attitude toward the woman.

Using stories and indirect questions may at times be the only effective way to confront people in a traditional society. An American who worked with refugee women in the Philippines, orienting them to the United States, related how she would often unknowingly offend these women. One day she was particularly frustrated because it was clear during a session that one woman,

Mina, was upset with her. After class she asked Mina to stay behind. The teacher went to the blackboard, drew two stick figure women, then said to Mina, pointing at the appropriate figures, "This woman thinks that this woman is angry at her. Is she right?" Mina turned to the blackboard and replied, "Yes, she is angry because this woman has insulted her by insinuating that she does not take care of her children properly." The discussion continued on the blackboard, with questions and answers being addressed to the stick figures. At the conclusion, each woman felt better at being able to express her feelings without giving offense. Personal questions were raised but indirectly so neither woman lost face.

Group versus Individual Learning

Another technique that helps traditional learners adapt to formal schooling is the utilization of group exercises. Jesus rarely addressed individuals when teaching; his stories and questions were almost always addressed to the crowd, to smaller social gatherings such as people sharing a meal, or to the twelve disciples. Jesus asked the Twelve, "Whom say ye that I am?" (Luke 9:20 KJV). "Ye" is the King James translation for the plural "you." Jesus posed his question to the group, and perhaps only Peter had the courage to respond.

Applying this technique, a teacher may pose questions that require group response rather than the usual individual response. For example:

Teacher: Class, can you tell me what 27 divided by 3 is?
Students (all together): Nine!

Even though not everyone in the class knows the answer, the wrong answers are drowned out in the chorus of correct ones, and the students answering incorrectly quickly change their answers to conform.

Western educators can change their classroom techniques to incorporate group-oriented learning in addition to individual-oriented learning. But because western teaching is predicated on the individual, western-trained teachers find this change difficult. African students do not. They find it easy to learn in groups. This is true of the Yapese as well. They do not like to do anything by themselves. They prefer to answer questions, take tests, and write papers as a group.

Western educators have incorporated group-oriented learning in western schools with mixed success. When faced with a grade that depends on the contributions of others, the most competitive students become frustrated, intense, and fearful that their grades will suffer because of weaker students in the group. One must be careful, however, not to stereotype all non-westerners as group oriented and all westerners as individual oriented. The variables that determine group or individual orientation are much more complex than they seem at first glance. For example, a Chinese classroom may have fifty to seventy students in it, and they may cooperate because of sheer numbers, but they may not have the aggregate social sense that Del Chinchen (1994) describes among Liberian students. Schooling for a Chinese student may still be a solitary struggle, whereas for the Liberian it is clearly a group effort.

Teaching in Multicultural Contexts

One final thought about the necessity of bridging cultures concerns the nature of the schools in which we teach. Many readers will be teaching in seminaries and Bible colleges in multicultural urban contexts, where both the faculty and students come from diverse cultural backgrounds. In such situations, we must be careful not to stereotype the students as learning in only one way. A teacher could conceivably have students from a dozen or more cultures in one classroom, and it is impossible to understand all the learning differences that those cultures represent. This is as true of my classroom in Southern California as it is of a classroom in Belgium.

For example, I teach a graduate course in social change. We wrestle with the economic implications of today's globalization, and I search for visual and kinesthetic ways to make the topics come alive. For some, throwing a beach ball back and forth to illustrate conflicting ideas about the environment seems childish and a waste of time. For others, they remember the argument *because* of the beach ball. One student who had taken the course on social change two semesters earlier astonished me when he recalled almost every week's topic by associating it with the visual/kinesthetic device I had used. The few weeks he could not remember were the weeks I had lectured and facilitated discussions.

Whether teaching in Los Angeles, New York City, Brussels, or Bangalore, you may be teaching a multicultural group of students. Even the elementary students I taught on Yap came from six different cultures. You may ask, How can a teacher become a 150-percent person in such diverse contexts? Which of the several cultures in my classroom should I choose to learn and adopt? Fortunately, cultures tend to share common value clusters. While Chinese, Japanese, and Korean cultures have many significant differences, they share a common Confucian heritage for family and educational values. A teacher who is committed to learning from his or her students will discover shared values that can become part of his or her teaching repertoire.

Teachers cannot possibly teach to all the potential differences, but they can become more culturally sensitive to the diversity of their students. One of the most important things they can do is explain the context of what they are doing and make their teaching techniques explicit. Nothing, however, substitutes for spending time with students in social situations in which they may feel freer to volunteer information that will inform teachers' planning. By listening, teachers can also gain their trust.

Research/Reflection Questions

1. How do your students interact with one another in class? Do they prefer to work together, answer questions together, and get the same grade? Make a list of things they do collectively and things they do individually. Compare.
2. If possible, observe both an American classroom and a non-western classroom. Make a simple form for yourself to record how often questions are used by either the teacher or the students and what types of questions they are. Do this more than once in order to have a basis for comparison.

five

Intelligence
and Learning Styles

In 1979, we shared the responsibility of teaching our son, Joel, a third grader, while we both conducted research on the island of Yap in Micronesia. Blending research work and teaching provided some unique challenges. I (Sherwood) assumed that Joel would be able to do his math and social science work on his own, with some coaching and checking by me. This did not work. He labored over the math problems I gave him, was often distracted, and finished only a handful of addition and subtraction problems in an hour. For a week or two I tried encouragement, harassment, and punishment to move him along faster in his work, all to no avail. Finally in desperation I sat down with him and asked him, "Ten minus four is what?" He responded instantly, "Six!" I tried again: "Nineteen minus seven is what?" Again he replied without hesitation, "Twelve." In the next ten minutes, Joel solved orally, without error, a full page of addition and subtraction problems in the textbook. Astounded at his proficiency, I decided to conduct all math lessons orally from that point on.

Over the next several months, we experimented with different techniques to discover how Joel learned most effectively. We noticed that handwriting was particularly difficult for him. He always struggled to complete a written assignment. But we found he was exceptionally adept at comprehending reading materials and solving ve.'bal math problems. We also noticed that his interest and learning comprehension jumped dramatically when we sat with him, as opposed to when he worked alone. We revised our strategy as teachers. We reduced the time of study from about four hours working alone with intermittent coaching to less than two hours working in dialogue with us. His learning progress increased dramatically. When we returned to New York near the end of the academic school year, Joel rejoined his third-grade class. His teacher reported that he was ahead of the class in all subjects except for writing.

Learning Styles

The way people process information is called their learning style. It is a cognitive strategy in which the brain sorts and categorizes new information. Rosalie Cohen (1969) is often credited with bringing the discussion of learning style into the schooling arena. Her research grew out of a concern over the continuing failure of African American students to perform as well as Anglo-Americans in school. She looked at the ways African American parents and children processed information and discovered that learning was almost exclusively relational. Cohen concluded that African American populations favor relational learning, while Anglo populations favor what she terms analytical learning. Following Cohen, other researchers coined terms such as "visual and verbal" and "global and dichotomous" (Mayers 1987) to describe these differences in learning styles.

The difference between these two styles lies in how people sort new information. Relational or global learners see the whole first, whereas analytical or dichotomous learners see the parts first, then relate them to the whole. Some cultures value and reward global strategies: learning by watching, by memorizing whole texts, or by participating in an activity. Other cultures value and reward verbal, analytical thinking, in which the learner asks exploratory questions or separates an object, a story, or an argument into its constituent parts. The analytical learner sorts and recombines the parts into new forms or poses alternative explanations and argues for or against them.

Some people mistakenly assume that all non-western people are global learners and all westerners are analytical. That is not the case because a learning style is an individual circumstance, not a cultural one. The case study of our son, Joel, suggests that he learns best in a relational context. Among the Yapese high school students I tested in 1980, most favored a global processing style, but some were clearly analytical in the way they sorted new information (J. E. Lingenfelter 1990). One particular student, Mike, was strongly analytical. He continued his schooling in the United States and did very well, but when he returned to Yap, he definitely did not fit in. He questioned everything, and Yapese people told me he was proud and uppity. They saw him as a young person who thought he knew everything and questioned the way things were done; he was not accepted because he posed a threat to the older to younger flow of knowledge.

Most scholars agree on a definition of intelligence that relates it to the ability to solve problems of increasing complexity in differing contexts (cf. Gardner 1983). This definition is preferable to the standard IQ (Intelligence Quotient), which measures only a student's ability to succeed in school and to do tasks appropriate for his or her grade level. Both Joel and Mike are intelligent young men, showing strong abilities to solve problems. Yet each lives in a culture that does not reward his particular learning style.

Jacqueline Goodnow (1990), in a provocative piece of research entitled "The Socialization of Cognition," states that people around the world not only learn to solve problems but also learn which problems are worth solving and which solutions are elegant rather than merely acceptable. She suggests that some particular pieces of knowledge are expected, others can be happily ignored, while still others are inappropriate for all but a few to own. Further, some ways of acquiring knowledge are more acceptable than others, and particular ways of seeking are expected for particular areas of knowledge. Her research reminds us of the importance of culture and reaffirms the importance of spending time observing a new context before beginning to teach in it.

Cultural Definitions of Intelligence

Several scholars have investigated differing cultural concepts of intelligence, and their insights can greatly aid educators in developing a more well-rounded understanding of a concept often merely equated with IQ. Robert Serpell (1993), a cognitive psychologist who lived in Zambia for over twenty years, engaged in a long-term study of the significance of schooling among the Chewa people. The Chewa declare that intelligence encompasses three domains: wisdom, cleverness, and responsibility. A person possessing one or two of them is not considered highly intelligent. Serpell illustrates the lack of true intelligence in the Brer Rabbit stories that made their way from Africa to America during the era of slavery and exaggerate cleverness without the other two virtues. While Brer Rabbit was clever, he was definitely not responsible. Serpell suggests that Chewa and other African people teach responsibility or trustworthiness by sending children on errands for adults. While some say this practice provides an efficient message system, Serpell argues that it is much more, because parents categorize intelligent children as "those willing to be sent." This sense of trustworthiness complements the dimensions of wisdom and cleverness, ideas that certainly parallel biblical teaching in the Book of Proverbs.

Howard Gardner (1983), another cognitive psychologist, set out to examine the idea of intelligence cross-culturally. Assuming that intelligence is broader than IQ, he examined hundreds of potential candidates for intelligence. Believing that the notion of intelligence as a single entity is too simplistic, he proposed the idea of "intelligences." The question then becomes "How are you smart?" rather than "How smart are you?" His most salient criteria for determining what constitutes an intelligence include:

1. the potential for isolation by brain damage (e.g., a particular capacity, such as language, could be destroyed or spared)

2. the existence of idiot savants, prodigies, and other exceptional individuals (e.g., in the film *Rain Man*, Dustin Hoffman's character was mentally incompetent in skills for daily life yet possessed an awesome mathematical ability; Mozart performed and wrote complex music as a child)
3. a critical ability to define flawed and flawless performance in specialized fields (e.g., the orchestra conductor Arturo Toscannini stopped a one-hundred piece orchestra during rehearsal to complain that one person played an F sharp instead of an F natural three bars earlier)
4. an identifiable "end-of-state" performance, or a performance that sets the standard for excellence (e.g., Michael Jordan's exceptional performances in NBA basketball championship games; Einstein's theory of relativity)

After much investigation, Gardner identified seven intelligences that occur worldwide:

1. linguistic, which represents the varied facets of language
2. musical, the essential components of which include pitch and rhythm (e.g., instrumentalists, vocalists, composers; Gardner says this intelligence surfaces perhaps the earliest of any)
3. logical/mathematical, which involves manipulation of the abstract world of logic (e.g., in the Liberian Kpelle game of O-Wa-Ree, players calculate over three hundred different moves; some mathematicians solve a problem just because they enjoy the challenge of manipulating numbers and producing something new and solvable)
4. spatial, which involves producing and manipulating forms (e.g., painters, interior designers, a Pulawat navigator who sails by stars, wind, and water)
5. bodily kinesthetic, which involves exceptional control of the body to perform difficult and complex tasks (e.g., Balinese dancers, a basketball player such as Shaquille O'Neal, and a mime such as Marcel Marceau)
6. internal personal, which involves access to one's own feelings (e.g., a philosopher or a mystic)
7. external personal, which encompasses the ability to discern the feelings, thoughts, and expectations of diverse

individuals and to engage them relationally in meaningful ways (e.g., a people-oriented pastor, counselor, or busi-
ness leader)

Note how only the linguistic and sometimes the external personal intelligences depend on verbal skills. The other five embrace a wide range of mental and bodily functions. Of the seven,
Gardner feels that the personal intelligences are of tremendous
importance in many if not all societies in the world, but they
have tended to be ignored or minimized by most students of
learning. Further, individuals usually possess several of these
intelligences in varying degrees. In recent years, Gardner has
added naturalistic intelligence to this list and is currently con-
sidering (I suspect under pressure) a ninth intelligence he calls
existential. I say "under pressure" because in his 1999 book,
Intelligence Reframed, he spends several pages explaining why
this is *not* an intelligence, a discussion that tells the reader more
about Gardner than about the intelligence.

The notion of "end-of-state" performance helps us better
understand the nature of each intelligence and its expression
across cultures. What does an end-of-state performance look
like in different cultures? In how many societies around the
world, for example, is music a strong part of the culture? Singers,
dancers, and those who play musical instruments all possess
musical intelligence to a certain degree. Mozart and Chopin are
two European musicians who represent end-of-state performance in their cultural milieu. How far this musical intelligence
is developed, however, depends on a combination of things. For
example, on Yap, people have no indigenous musical instruments, and parents teach children that singing is inappropriate
except during the performance of traditional dances. While some
Yapese children may have a genetic capacity for a highly developed musical intelligence, their parents do not encourage or
reward them for musical performance. The singers (who provide the only music for a Yapese dance) learned the skill by listening, singing along in group contexts, and emerging as experts
in their middle-age years after the eldest singers had died. Among
these middle-age singers, Yapese readily identify the end-of-state
performers. By way of contrast, the Javanese in Indonesia, where
dance and music constitute the daily fabric of their lives, encour-

age their children to participate in dance, singing, and instrumental performances, developing this intelligence at a much younger age.

Each of the seven intelligences confers problem-solving and performance abilities, the combination of which varies from person to person, and each person exercises intelligence in distinct ways. We have a friend whose external personal intelligence is the closest to end-of-state we have observed. He has demonstrated a marvelous ability to relate to diverse people all over the world. We have never seen him make a cultural mistake that he did not quickly recognize and apologize for or correct. After he retired and moved to Florida, he told us that he had had to prepare himself mentally for the move, because he knew that getting to know an entirely new group of people would take a great deal of energy, and he was not sure he could do it again. While most of us think of a move in terms of housing, he focused entirely on the interpersonal issues.

Gardner's astute observations of the relationships between mind and body have helped us understand the complexity of God's capstone work of creation—the human species, male and female. Unfortunately, however, Gardner's theory of intelligences does not include moral, character, or spiritual elements, and he does not consider responsibility or trustworthiness. Gardner's western scientific bias about knowledge and intelligence tends to separate and compartmentalize what Serpell says is part of a unified whole.

Adapting Teaching to Student Learning

Unlike Gardner, we begin with the assumption that God has created people in his image, and therefore, we reflect in part the mind of God. Scripture teaches that God has created us body and soul or body, mind, and spirit. As already demonstrated, as prisoners of our cultures, we distort God's creative work and his purpose and meaning for humanity. In western cultures, part of that distortion has involved giving priority to the analytical learning style (see table 5.1 and chap. 3), elevating the linguistic and logical/mathematical intelligences above the others, and denying the moral/spiritual dimension of God's creative work.

Table 5.1

Learning Styles and the Intelligences Valued

Traditional Learning	Formal Schooling
Relational Learning Style	**Analytical Learning Style**
Visual	Verbal
Global	Dichotomous
Example	Question
Narrative	Proposition
Valued Intelligences	**Valued Intelligences**
External personal	Linguistic
Spatial	Logical/mathematical
Bodily kinesthetic	Musical
	Internal personal

The culture of western schooling is based on that distortion and thus has elevated the propositional style of teaching and devalued relational learning in the classroom. Non-western cultures, in their distortion of creation, give priority to the relational learning style and the associated external personal, spatial, and bodily kinesthetic intelligences.

Roland Allen (1930) and Charles Kraft (1983, 1999) have shown how this distortion pervaded Christian witness, mission, and mission education in the nineteenth and twentieth centuries. Kraft (1999, 33–54) pleads that we correct this distortion and adopt the methods that Jesus used for communication in the church and the classroom. He notes that Jesus used parables and stories to teach the crowds and train his disciples. Jesus also took his disciples with him, sharing every aspect of his life and ministry. They walked together, ate together, watched him teach, participated with him in his miracles, prayed together, and slept together in homes, along the road, and in the Garden of Gethsemane. After an extended period of watching, listening, and participating with him in ministry, Jesus sent them out in twos to practice the things they had seen him do.

A careful study of Jesus' practice shows a blend of relational and analytical techniques for teaching his disciples and the others who followed him. His method of choice was the parable, and his preferred teaching context was relational. He told his students, "Follow me." But he often answered a question with another question, pushed people beyond their accepted categories, and forced them to analyze their teaching and practices. At times he lectured, and sometimes he preached. His exams were usually painfully practical: "Go! . . . Do not take a purse or bag or sandals. . . . Heal the sick who are there and tell them, 'The kingdom of God is near you'" (Luke 10:3–4, 9). "Sell everything you have and give to the poor. . . . Then come, follow me" (Luke 18:22).

The challenge for cross-cultural teachers is to break out of the cultural boxes that have limited teaching and learning to a select few of the God-given intelligences. We often see another's culture of teaching and learning as deficient and think of our own culture as superior. As Christian teachers we know we should "consider others better than ourselves" (Phil. 2:3), yet we are convinced of the superiority of our training and gifts. As teachers we must begin as learners—observing carefully the diverse blends of intelligences in our students and the diversity of cultural ways in which they have become accustomed to learning.

Earle and Dorthy Bowen (1986), studying Kenyan student learning, concluded that a high percentage of these students learned best when teachers employed relational learning strategies. They have suggested a number of practical classroom tactics to help the non-western educator utilize relational strategies in the classroom (see table 5.2).

Cynthia Tobias (1994) has observed that some students learn much better when their bodily kinesthetic intelligence is engaged. These students cannot sit still; they must be moving to remain focused on a learning task. Other students must talk to learn. Still others learn best through music or visual stimulation. Some learn best in solitude and reflection.

The Gospels document the way in which Jesus engaged his disciples in all these learning contexts. Luke records that he taught while they were on the road, traveling to Jerusalem, or on a plain where people could sit, stand, play, or talk to one another while they listened. Jesus often used teachable moments, using a life situation in which he and his audience were participants, to provoke learning (Luke 14). Many times his lesson was in the

Table 5.2

Suggestions for Effective Teaching Methods with Relational Sensitive African Students

1. Provide a course outline
2. Give an oral preview of the entire course
3. Preview the material to be learned in each individual lesson
4. Specify the important points in a lesson
5. Provide frequent feedback and reinforcement
6. Give small units of work rather than large ones
7. Recognize that relational students are much more sensitive to praise or criticism from others
8. Let students work in groups
9. Provide structure and direction when assigning a project
10. Provide a textbook or duplicated notes
11. Use visual aids of all kinds
12. Use external rather than internal motivators
13. Use visual models and examples
14. Let students do things in their own way
15. Supplement lectures with handouts, pictures, etc.
16. Use material that is socially oriented (related to people or situations)
17. Use criterion-referenced grading
18. Teach coping strategies for dealing with methods that seem strange to students

(Bowen 1988, 8–11)

form of a conversation, such as the one he had with Simon the Pharisee when a prostitute washed Jesus' feet with her tears. He used word pictures for those who think in pictures, and poetic parallelisms for those who love words and the logic of language. Solitude, reflection, and prayer were learning disciplines that he shared with those who were closest to him.

But how can we bring these diverse strategies into classrooms in which a culture of schooling already defines student and teacher expectations? Many U.S. educators have already embraced Gardner's work and seek to train students in more than just the linguistic and mathematical intelligences. The challenge is to engage the other intelligences in a manner that does not violate the hidden curriculum of schooling. For example, a teacher could cover all the "expected" pedagogical strategies in the classroom and then invite the students to her home, where they could put on a play using the concepts from the classroom.

The evening would be social, and food and fellowship the stated purpose. Having the students dramatize course concepts would further cement those concepts in their minds, because it would allow the other intelligences to surface and be recognized.

The key principles in the foregoing discussion lie in the understanding that God has wired each brain differently. Researchers attempt to identify patterns that allow teachers to help each student learn most effectively. No one teacher can accommodate all the possible intelligences and learning styles, but this chapter should help stimulate a teacher's creativity in the methods of presenting new material.

Research/Reflection Questions

1. Ask the parents of your students to name a person in their own cultural group who they think is smart. Ask them to provide examples of things they have observed in this person that led them to this conclusion.
2. Find out how young people learn new skills from others. Observe someone learning to weave, garden, repair a truck engine, etc.
3. Experiment with having students over to your home to dramatize course concepts. Discuss the experience with the students, perhaps in class the next time you meet.

six

The Role of the Teacher

Several years ago I taught in a university extension program in Asia. I was one of several American professors who rotated through the program, which was based on two- or three-week intensive courses. My first year there I was very conscious of the hierarchical nature of schooling, and I used the lecture format as my main teaching method. As the various American professors cycled through the program, however, a curious change occurred among the students. They began to enjoy the more interactive style of some of the professors and embraced it with delight. However, when I returned for the third time to teach, the students' respect patterns had changed dramatically. While they had embraced a more open classroom style and had jettisoned their cultural patterns, they had not learned the patterns of control and discipline that make this style viable. I felt we had failed them by substituting one teaching style for another without also providing a corresponding understanding of its cultural rules and constraints.

People who teach cross-culturally encounter differences in the expectations students have of the way in which teachers should conduct themselves in the classroom. My cultural heritage often conflicts with the ethnic backgrounds of my students, provoking clashes over items such as handing in homework or answering questions. When I taught a group of African American students in McKeesport, I felt like an outsider. In Africa, colleagues tell us that students expect them to be surrogate parents.

One contrast of teaching styles is Confucian versus western. In their research in Hong Kong, John Flowerdew and Lindsay Miller (1995, 348) found that students who embrace the Confucian ethic expect a teacher to be an authority who is never questioned. Confucian family values motivate students to excel, and they are oriented toward group achievement. In contrast, western students expect a teacher to be a guide who can be challenged. They are motivated by individual desire and emphasize individual development. While this comparison offers some valid insights, it reduces the complexity of culture to "us versus them." All Asian societies are not alike, any more than all western societies are alike. However, this contrast in teaching styles provides a good starting place for discussion.

Patricia Furey (1986, 20), when examining the teaching of English in cross-cultural contexts, discovered that teachers act out diverse roles such as sage/scholar, counselor/advisor, tutor, and patron. She also noted that differences in individualism and group orientation strongly affected the receptivity of students toward their teacher. How does a teacher analyze the cultural context of the classroom in which he or she is teaching to determine *when* he or she should expect to be seen as a sage/scholar, a counselor/advisor, a tutor, or a patron?

The Social Contexts of Teaching

The opening discussion of hidden curriculum showed that schooling always occurs in a much larger cultural context. To be effective, teachers must learn how that context shapes their role, their students' role, and the dynamics of teaching and learning. At first this seems a formidable task! People can spend years trying to learn a language and a culture and only approximate the expertise of those who learn them as children. Thankfully, anthropologists have developed tools for cross-cultural learning that help speed up this process and focus on the specific aspects of culture essential to the teaching task.

Because schools are public, part of a wider community, and children come from family contexts to schools, the logical place to begin is to seek to understand the nature of family and community for students. In my (Sherwood's) earlier work (Lingenfelter 1996, 1998), I developed research tools that one can employ to discover the essential elements of family and community. Here we will use the same comparative framework to illuminate the different social contexts of teaching and learning.

The first variable one must seek to understand is the degree to which a society values conformity to the collective or group expectations of family and community. In the Confucian-western contrast noted above, students from Confucian families work under the pressure of parental expectations, and a sense of family honor is at stake. If they do well, the family and the student are honored and pleased. If they do poorly, the family and the student suffer shame, and the student withdraws in shame from the group. The student's quest for learning and achievement is directly linked to the honor and expectations of the family. Students from western cultures do not share this collective burden. While most respect their families, their motivation to learn comes from their personal interests and objectives. While parents may exert individual pressure on students to learn, the family and community offer little if any collective pressure for conformity. Each individual achieves honor alone and competes against others for personal recognition in the schooling context.

The second variable of importance is the degree to which a culture values the separation and specialization of roles and assigns high or low status to those roles. A Confucian teacher, for example, has a special and highly respected role, located among other high status positions in society. The teacher has authority, and therefore, a student would never question the teacher's word. The teacher is absolutely respected, and as a result, students always stand when the teacher enters the classroom, bow in deference, and listen carefully, writing word for word what the teacher says. A western teacher's role can vary widely. Western teachers of children have authority and demand respect, but they encourage questions from students and may even tolerate argument. Teachers of teens and adults often take a "peer expert" role, seeing the students as peers who lack a teacher's expertise but who are partners in the teaching and learning process. The cultural contrast is in the degree of separation and status. Both western and Confucian teachers have specialized roles and authority, but a Confucian teacher has a much higher status and degree of separation from his or her students.

Each society must define its social relationships with reference to these two variables. People must choose whether to value individual autonomy, conformity to a group, or a blend of these extremes. They must also decide whether individual roles will be broadly defined and open to all, narrowly defined and limited to a few select individuals, or a blend of these extremes. Each variable may be described as a continuum—weak to strong demands for conformity to a group and weak to strong differentiation of social roles and status.

When these two variables are considered together in a matrix, they define four distinctive social types, or prototype social games (see fig. 6.1). We use the term "social game" for several reasons. First, as with games that we play for fun, people can participate in more than one, with differing degrees of interest and commitment. Second, these types can be learned, expanded, adapted, and changed according to the will of the players. Third, people can be extremely serious about a social game, treating it as if their lives depended on it, or they can be quite casual and even disinterested participants. Finally, the analogy of a game is useful because the structure of play parallels the structure of more serious social relationships.

Each social context, or game, has a different set of rules and expectations, and participants must play according to those rules to be accepted and effective. For example, in the social context of American schools, students do not expect teachers to act like parents and may resent it if they do. However, in the context of family, children, while they may be proud that their parents are teachers, want them to baby-sit the grandchildren and keep their marriage relationship on a firm footing.

Strong, cohesive groups distinguish the hierarchist and egalitarian social games. Strong groups have clearly defined boundaries and sharp insider/outsider distinctions. The survival of the group is more important than the survival of an individual, and

Figure 6.1

Four Prototype Social Games

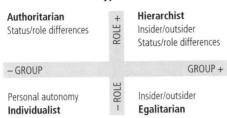

one's identity is found in the group. Youth gangs exemplify the strong group value. Members must go through rites of passage to enter the group, wear common clothing, talk a certain way, and support one another whenever called upon. In some gangs, the only way out is death.

In contrast, American university classes represent an example of a weak group (authoritarian and individualist social games). The classes are open to anyone who has been admitted to the program and can pay the tuition. Students feel no obligation to one another beyond that of suffering through the same class together. They dress according to the weather, occasionally forget to turn in assignments, and do not expect to maintain a continuing relationship with other students beyond the class. While group relationships exist, they are not highly valued and are not allowed to interfere with individual autonomy.

The authoritarian and hierarchist social games are characterized by a strong differentiation of status and role. One may be the oldest son in a Chinese family, or the only one with a Ph.D. from a small African village, or the president of a major South American corporation. Each of these roles has certain characteristics: The social system elaborates the expectations for each role, the roles are closed so that only one or a few may enter, and they are restrictive so that individuals must fulfill the expectations associated with the role. One's age, gender, title, parents, wealth, and so on determine how one relates to everyone else. For example, one does not expect a Korean pastor of a large church to serve the traditional tea to visitors; that is the

Figure 6.2

Four Prototype Teacher Roles

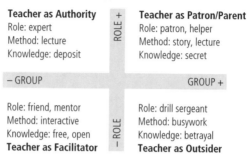

Teacher as Authority	ROLE +	**Teacher as Patron/Parent**
Role: expert		Role: patron, helper
Method: lecture		Method: story, lecture
Knowledge: deposit		Knowledge: secret
– GROUP		**GROUP +**
Role: friend, mentor		Role: drill sergeant
Method: interactive		Method: busywork
Knowledge: free, open	–ROLE	Knowledge: betrayal
Teacher as Facilitator		**Teacher as Outsider**

job of a female assistant. A person working on the ground crew at a university would not issue checks; that is the job of the chief financial officer. People know where they fit.

The individualist and egalitarian social games do not emphasize roles. Status and role differences may be evident, but people minimize these differences. Instead, personal giftedness is highly valued. When people do assume roles, the roles are usually positions that are open to anyone who feels inclined and gifted to assume them.

The culture of a school often, but not always, reflects the social preferences of the wider community in which it is located. In a community in which a version of the authoritarian social game holds sway, the school will likely be structured similarly, and the role of the teacher will be that of an authority figure. If, on the other hand, a community embraces the individualist social game, its school will likely allow much more individual freedom, and the teacher will be a facilitator. Figure 6.2 illustrates the role of the teacher in each of the four prototype social games.

Teacher as Facilitator or Authority

American schools tend to value individual freedom, and teachers most often work in a facilitator role. The methods used in the classroom include lecture but also emphasize the importance of student dialogue and interaction. Students are the focus, and teachers expect them to contribute to the learning process. Because knowledge is open to anyone, the teacher is not the final expert; students may at times challenge and disagree with him or her. Student perceptions of teachers vary according to students' subjective assessments of how well the teacher does his or her job, and they do not hesitate to criticize when they feel the teacher has not done it well. While American middle-class students recognize their professors as such, status is de-emphasized. Often graduate students address professors by their first names rather than by their last.

However, this role contrasts sharply with the expectations many Asian students have for their teachers. Coming from families and church communities that are authoritarian or hierarchist, they do not expect teachers to be wrong or to admit it when they are. They prefer lectures, because then they can take notes. They also prefer receiving a handout of the lecture in advance so they will not miss a word. They expect teachers to deposit knowledge into their "banks," and they will receive it obediently. They maintain a high respect for the position of college professor, using only titles and last names to show their respect. They expect teachers to wear formal clothing, even though they dress more casually. These students bring their authoritarian expectations to class.

The expectations of students who see the teacher as an authority figure contrast sharply with the expectations of students who see the teacher as a facilitator (see fig. 6.3). Students who see the teacher as an authority figure do not value independent thinking; they merely want the teacher to tell them what will be on the test so they can memorize it. When the teacher tries to encourage questions and interaction, the students often feel it is a waste of time. Every classroom has its distinctive social game, and conflicts arise when students and teachers bring different social game expectations to the classroom.

Pamela George, whose book *College Teaching Abroad* (1995) surveys Fulbright scholars who have taught in various countries around the world, summarizes the frustrations they experienced. While many of the frustrations were related to inadequate resources, others related to the actual teaching process. For example:

Figure 6.3

Four Prototype Learner Roles

I would say, "What about this?" And then I'd wait. I'd sit there and sip my tea. . . . Nothing. Then I'd call on somebody, "Chung, what do you think?" He would look down at his book . . . [silence] . . . [silence]. I have no experience with this—the experience of calling on a student and the ability of that student to outwait me! (A Syracuse University Professor, China) (14)

This professor, working from the teacher as facilitator role, expected interaction with his students. He expected them to ask questions or at least to answer when called upon. The students, however, reared in a tradition in which status is important and the teacher is the authority, were unfamiliar with that pattern. They were in class to learn from the professor, and the only questions they expected to answer were those that had clear right or wrong answers.

Either of these roles may be used against students. The facilitator may use student interaction to avoid preparation so as to spend time writing for publication or on other personal interests. The authoritarian teacher can scar a student with verbal or physical abuse. Several years ago I had a Taiwanese student in a doctoral program who was so scared in class that she literally went home crying after each session. Much later she was able to tell me of her traumatic experiences as a young child in Taiwan and how the teachers beat students who did not do as well as expected on tests.

Teacher as Patron/Parent

A third role that teachers may take in formal schooling settings around the world is patron/parent. This typically occurs when the hierarchist social game is highly valued, conformity to a kin or community group is important, and leadership is hierarchical. Some African and Asian doctoral students who have come from such cultural settings to Fuller Theological Seminary refer to their male faculty mentors as their "father." They hold and affirm this relationship until the mentor dies. The student expects his mentor to care for him the way a father cares for a son, helping him when he has financial needs, giving him guidance on personal as well as academic matters, and creating a path for the student to enter a professional career or ministry. The obligations of such a role are sometimes lost on the faculty members, who are often surprised by the requests and expectations of their students.

Other students from hierarchist social settings may not employ the kinship role but describe their teacher as a patron. The patron-client relationship expresses an alliance between two persons of unequal status, power, or resources, each of whom finds it useful to have as an ally, someone superior or inferior. The superior member is called the patron, the inferior the client. The patron gives protection, social access, and material assistance to the client. The client reciprocates with respect, loyalty, and service. At its best, such a relationship is reciprocal and works to the benefit of both participants. The focus of patron-client relationships, relationships typically found in post-colonial schools in which most of the students are poor, is on wealth in people, not in banks. Maintaining reciprocal relationships takes priority with people who know they cannot trust an unstable political government or a constantly fluctuating currency. Many western teachers reject the patron role because they do not wish to engage in this obligatory reciprocity, having seen only its abuses, not its strengths.

Del Chinchen (1994) found that the African students he taught relied constantly on patron-client relationships. When he first resisted becoming a patron, his students felt he was personally rejecting them. He worried about the potential for corruption, and he did not want to feel indebted to anyone. But as he learned more about these relationships, he realized that to the African, wealth lies in people, not in things. The patron-client system was rooted in a belief that knowledge is power and personal. Those who have knowledge keep it secret, giving it only to clients with whom they have a relationship. An African phrase that best expresses this says, "I am because we are." Chinchen's African students believed that school was a struggle, endurable if a social one but cruel if a solitary one.

When students see the teacher as a parent or a patron, the teacher becomes the gateway to opportunity. If students do well, they may go farther. A student learns because of a relationship, and the teaching methods—such as oral storytelling, lecture, call and response, and humor—affirm the parent or patron bond with the student. Student expectations of the teacher are high, and the student does not want to disappoint the teacher. If the system works well, the teacher gives knowledge and the student gives respect. The focus is clearly on the importance of establishing relationships in order to learn.

Western teachers often reject the parent or patron role because they see it as a never ending demand for them to give to students without reciprocity. Because most westerners understand "giving" only in a material sense, they miss the opportunity to establish relationships that enhance their respect and honor in a community and that give students a sense of security. In volatile political and economic situations, the notion of having wealth in people is more important than any other kind of wealth.

Teacher as Outsider

The egalitarian social game creates two contrasting roles for teachers. When a teacher is located within a strong group context, he or she plays the role of elder sibling, an insider whose goal is cultural continuity. When a teacher is located outside the group, members see the teacher as a threat to their values and identity. The role of teacher as outsider presents the greatest challenge for effective teaching.

My second teaching job was in a steel mill town in western Pennsylvania. My students were mostly African American, the time was the 1960s, and the mood was decidedly hostile between blacks and whites. As a young, enthusiastic teacher, I could not understand the hostility of my lower-income African American students, because I did not feel I had done anything to warrant it. What I did not understand was that I was an outsider because of socioeconomic forces beyond my control. I was pressured by the administration and the students into a role similar to that of a drill sergeant, clearly in command but with a passively aggressive group of students.

Harry Wolcott (1987), who wrote about his first experience teaching among the Kwakiutl Indians in the Northwest Territories, found himself in a similar situation. Wolcott wrote that the only thing his students wanted to get out of school was to get out of school. They preferred lectures and busywork, not activities that engaged their minds and hearts. They saw learning the "white man's stuff" as a betrayal of their Indian identity and the teacher as their enemy.

Dumbfounded by this response, Wolcott sought an explanation in the wider cultural context. The school, run by white mission or government employees, often denigrated the Indian students' values, ways of life, and language. The students had learned to cope through minimal compliance—doing enough to pass, be promoted, and get out. But they did not expect to learn. School was a necessary evil. They were forced to go, but they were determined not to learn the white man's ways.

When a teacher is an outsider, the focus of the role is control. The teacher must control the class to teach, while the students resist, defying the teacher's efforts to get them to learn. This is in direct contrast to a patron-client relationship, in which students learn *because of* a relationship. When the teacher is an outsider, the students refuse to allow a relationship. The group functions differently in these two social contexts. In the hierarchist social game, the teacher is brought into the group and is expected to play the roles assigned by the group (e.g., respected elder). In the egalitarian social game in which the teacher is an outsider, the students form a group against the teacher. The unfortunate consequence of this opposition is that the teacher may hate the students, or the students may hate the teacher.

Because egalitarians reject outsiders, western educators may have no choice but to recruit teachers who are insiders. An insider begins with trust and can teach in a way that maintains the integrity and identity of the group. An Amish teacher in an Amish school or a Muslim imam in a Muslim village school are examples. The instructional methods vary with the religious traditions, but the goals of learning are cultural continuity, not betrayal. The students become stronger members of the group and follow the teacher as an expert in the traditions of the group. However, such teachers have little if any interest in new knowledge and usually teach students to be suspicious of the outside world and change. They are often ineffective in helping students become effective participants in a wider community of relationships.

Rethinking Your Teaching Role

This chapter has shown that students from different social contexts bring to the classroom different expectations about the role of the teacher and their participation as students in the learning process. It has also shown that western teachers have often misunderstood those contexts, judged them inadequate or dysfunctional, and sought to impose their own forms of teaching and learning on their students. At times they have succeeded, but more often their efforts have led to frustration and sometimes despair for both teacher and students. To be an effective teacher across cultures, you must rethink the role you play in the classroom and add new dimensions to your identity and practice. The goal is to envision yourself as a 150-percent person.

The first step for effective cross-cultural teaching is learning, becoming aware of the culture of others. What social values do students bring to schooling? How do they reflect the social games of their families and communities? How do they view you, the teacher, and themselves as students? As Patricia Furey says (1986, 20), our anger and frustration would be spared if we were aware of how differently our students see us. In the process of learning about others, we also begin to see ourselves more clearly. The model of prototype social games helps us see others and ourselves in the important dimensions of status/role and conformity to the pressures of a group.

The second step is self-awareness—learning who we are, what we value, and what social game preferences we hold. When Chinchen began to take the patron-client game of his African students seriously, he recognized his desire for independence, his resistance to indebtedness, and his reluctance to take on a "big man" role. He preferred to be a facilitator of learners and to have students as peer novices rather than as clients. He became aware that these were selfish interests that allowed him to remain in his comfort zone rather than to meet his students in their need. This realization moved Chinchen to take the next step, to form incarnational relationships with his students, to become a patron.

The incarnational teacher is willing to give up aspects of the teacher role that fits his or her cultural background and to take on the role that fits the social and cultural world of the students. For Chinchen (1994), this meant giving up the role of teacher as facilitator and taking on the role of teacher as patron. This was not an easy task. Chinchen first had to learn what was expected of a patron and the patterns of interaction that signaled a student's interest in being a client. He had to learn how to make the students play by their own rules and how to hold them to cultural standards of appropriate behavior and accountability. He had to deal with his own fears and anxiety about learning a new role and his distress at giving up familiar patterns of teaching. He made mistakes and in the beginning did not perform well in his emerging relationships or in his teaching. But over time his understanding of the game improved, and his performance pleased his students and him.

But Chinchen realized that the patron role was not adequate for his objectives as a Christian. He looked for ways to redeem the sometimes corrupt patron-client role and to turn it into a biblically founded role of teacher as discipler within the patron-client context. Over several years of learning and changing, he mentored a cohort of students in Liberia and Malawi who were deeply committed to him and to the school, which became their family and Christian community.

There are times when an incarnational approach may be exceedingly difficult if not impossible. When the local game is egalitarian, the group may resist a teacher's every effort to become an insider. In such a situation, Jesus sets for us an example of engagement. While he was excluded from groups such as the Pharisees, he accepted invitations to eat with them and to engage them in dialogue on issues. He respected them but also challenged them in areas in which their behavior contradicted their expressed values. Drawing on a deep knowledge of Scripture, he taught from the wisdom and integrity of his person. Working from divine character and compassion, he had a profound impact on those who listened to him. While he never became an insider to the Pharisees, many believed in him because of his person and message.

Sometimes we may find it impossible to learn and adopt parts of the expected role. What do we do then with student expectations? Sometimes we just need to make our role and rules explicit. We cannot assume that the students know what to expect in a classroom; we must tell them. Other times we may need to negotiate. One teacher we know elicits the students' expectations and states her own, and together they agree on the compromises necessary. The most important element is to recognize that as teachers we need to be learners. In the final analysis, our focus may encompass all four teaching roles. We need to communicate knowledge to students with whom we may or may not build a relationship, and we need to control the class in some fashion so that all can learn.

Research/Reflection Questions

1. If at all possible, arrange to observe a national colleague as he or she teaches a class. (Ask the principal to recommend someone who is an excellent teacher, and always ask permission of the teacher and explain why you want to observe.) Note differences between the way he or she conducts class and the way you do, then reflect on areas of discontinuity. Are there things you feel you do better? Are there things your colleague does better? What kinds of changes might you make?

2. Using table 6.1, identify the reciprocity expectations in the context in which you are teaching. (The table comes from an African context, but it is included here because it suggests some things you may not have thought of, especially those labeled "intangible.")

Table 6.1

Types of Patron-Client Relationship Gifts

Tangible	Intangible
Gifts from Patrons	**Gifts from Patrons**
1. money	1. advice, counsel
2. loans, credit	2. future aid guarantee
3. job	3. influence and prestige
4. dining companionship	4. extra time
5. telephone call	5. sponsorship
6. correspondence by letter	6. displayed sincerity
7. hospitality	7. interest
8. clothes, shoes, etc.	8. concern of welfare
9. visits	9. neutralization of competition, conflict, or danger
10. attendance at ceremonies	10. protection, defense, support
	11. settlement of disputes
	12. arrangement of apprenticeships
	13. contacts with creditors
Gifts from Clients	**Gifts from Clients**
1. labor, services	1. mandate to lead, acceptance of followership
2. chicken, goat, eggs	2. respect
3. garden vegetables, fruit	3. risk of life
4. token money	4. continuous display of affection, deference, and obedience
5. letter of thanks	5. loyalty, support, acclaim
6. cooked food	6. friendship
7. visits	7. protection, defense
	8. assistance in managing transactions with other clients

(Chinchen 1994, 156) Used by permission.

seven

Teaching for Change

In 1998, a strange sight took place on a hilly back street in Seoul. Ninety women and ten men, linked in groups of seven and eight, stumbled out into the street. All in each group were blindfolded except the leader. Cars stopped and schoolchildren stared. After approximately five minutes of parading up and down the hill, they returned to the classroom. With much laughter they began talking about their experience. Within a few short minutes, however, the mood turned solemn as their leader, a prominent Korean woman, led them to reflect on what they had learned and how it related to following leaders in their churches.

These participants all lived and worked in a context in which the teacher is the authority and lecture is the norm. However, the leader felt that the lecture format was limited in its ability to get at the affective components of the material under consideration. Because she was trying to help them build stronger marriages and families, she had invited me to join her in an experimental course in which we would use interactive learning techniques rather than traditional lecture.

As the professor and doctoral mentor of this woman, I found the entire experience overwhelming. I had entered into the week with some trepidation. Would an intentional experiential curriculum work in Korea? My Korean colleague was excited about trying it and had invited me to Seoul to guide her in the development of a four-day course on interpersonal relationships employing experiential teaching techniques. These adult students processed their reactions to each activity with amazing insights. In regard to the group "blind walk" exercise, for example, one woman wrote poignantly, "I didn't know how hard it was being the leader. . . . I need to have more patience as a follower!" The experiences, followed by intense debriefing, allowed participants to process their emotions in a way that lecture could not. The depth and emotion that surfaced as a result of the experiential approach convinced the leader that she needed to make experiential learning a regular part of her teaching.

Why Teach for Change?

When and why should teachers try to bring about change in the lives of their students? Throughout this book we have argued that the best strategies for teaching cross-culturally incorporate the hidden curriculum and cultural practices of the learners. We have shown that students learn best when they can do so within the familiar context of their own culture. Yet we have also acknowledged that cultures are prisons and that all people are in bondage to their culture. These prisons are often dysfunctional places and sometimes trap us in sinful and destructive patterns of behavior. It was precisely for this reason that the leader mentioned above engaged a group of Korean Christian leaders in experiential learning exercises.

Traditional Korean culture had a strong authoritarian division of labor between men and women. Marriages were arranged between families, and wives became subjects of their husbands and mothers-in-law, serving at their bidding and pleasure. Men and their mothers often used their authority over the wife in an abusive manner. In an agricultural context, people lived and worked together in extended families that centered around an elder man and his married sons. In the modern Korean context, nearly 30 percent of Koreans are Christians, and the vast majority of them live and work in modern cities. No longer living in extended families, husbands and wives face the economic and social pressures of the city alone. Yet they bring to Christian marriages the traditional pattern of male authority and domination, which all too often is abusive. Even among Christian leaders, wives often feel subjugated, unloved, and extremely unhappy.

The purpose of the experiential learning seminar in 1998 was to help Korean women, and a few willing men, confront these dysfunctional patterns in their families and cultural practices and empower them to change these patterns in a manner consistent with the teachings of Scripture and their faith. Based on their reading of Scripture and teaching in the church, they knew that husbands should love their wives and that wives should respect their husbands. But, caught in their traditionally rooted habits of domination and passive resistance, many Christian husbands abused their wives, and the wives in turn deeply resented their husbands.

The power of experiential learning lies in experience, having learners reflect on the experience and through that reflection make decisions about changing their thinking and behavior. We used these same techniques in Africa in 2000 in a workshop on partnership between missionary and national leaders. Parallel to the situation in Korea, Christian leaders found themselves locked in dysfunctional relationships and behaviors that were detrimental to their personal well-being and destructive to their ministries. The goal of the workshop was to help these Christian workers face their habitual behaviors, reflect on them from a biblical perspective, and then work together to bring about changes in their relationships and ministries.

When and why should we teach for change? We need cultural stability and continuity for personal and communal well-being. But whenever the habits and practices of our social and economic relationships become obstacles to the fundamental values and goals we hold as people, we must teach for change. As Christians, we seek to measure our lives and ministries against the standards set forth in the teaching of the Master, Jesus Christ. While we recognize that we always fall short of these standards, we need to strive continually to be transformed into the likeness of Christ. Experiential learning is one of the most powerful tools available to us to teach for change.

The Components of Experiential Learning

Experiential learning is a technical name for what people have been doing for hundreds of years. John Dewey discussed the links between education and experience during the early part of the twentieth century. Educators in the 1970s and 1980s followed Dewey and focused on teaching and learning through real or simulated experiences. Experiential learning encompasses a wide range of teaching and learning strategies, from apprenticeships to field projects, field trips, simulations, games, and so on, and it allows a greater latitude in the exercise of the multiple intelligences. While lecture has been the teaching method of choice in higher education for many reasons, students take in information passively and utilize only their linguistic and logical/mathematical intelligences in the form of tests and papers.

The two key components of experiential learning are doing and reflecting on what happened. Having an experience is not in itself enough. The Korean woman's experience of leading a group of blindfolded women did not lead to new understanding until she reflected on her experience as both leader and follower. With some help from the teacher and feedback from those who had followed her, she began to make connections between her experience as a follower in church and the experience of those who had to follow her in the blind walk. Through her experience as a leader, feedback from followers, and reflection, she gained a new appreciation for the difficulty involved in leading effectively in a different context, her church.

David Kolb (1984) describes learning as a process whereby knowledge is created through the transformation of experience. Building on the work of Kurt Lewin (1957) and Jean Piaget (1970), he constructed a simple circular model to illustrate how knowledge is created. Learning begins with concrete experience, such as the blind walk of the Korean adults, followed by reflective observation, as illustrated in the Korean group's debriefing of their blind walk experiences. Reflective observations should lead to the formation of abstract generalizations—in the Korean case, principles that the learner can use to guide his or her behavior and feelings in following leaders. The last phase of the circle Kolb called active experimentation. After experiencing, reflecting, and abstracting, one tries again with new insights.

Figure 7.1

Experiential Learning

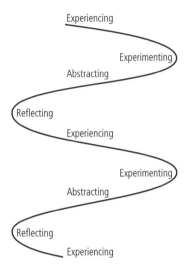

Experiencing

Experimenting

Abstracting

Reflecting

Experiencing

Experimenting

Abstracting

Reflecting

Experiencing

While one could stay stuck in an endless circle, the idea behind Kolb's model is that one moves to higher levels as one solves problems of increasing complexity. The model then looks more like a steep circular staircase (see fig. 7.1).

The Korean leader chose experiential learning techniques to help Korean women break out of traditional patterns of relating that had become dysfunctional. The activities employed had the intentional purpose of creating dissonance, or a feeling of discomfort, in the participants. After proceeding through the discomfort phase, they reflected on the source of the discomfort. When people recognize the causes of their discomfort, they are more capable of finding ways to change their behaviors, thereby reducing discomfort or dissonance. It is not until one experiences the involvement, the dissonance, and the reflection that learning actually takes place.

A personal example may help make this clear. In the summer of 1993, I spent several weeks in the town of Waterloo, south of Brussels in Belgium. I lived by myself in an apartment. Down the street was a supermarket where I could buy food. My French was limited to only a few phrases, but I knew how to shop in a super-market, so I figured I would be okay. I went to the market a few times and was able to navigate quite well without any significant problems. Then came the day I decided to buy a tomato. They looked wonderful: big, fat, red tomatoes piled high. I selected a tomato, put it in a little plastic bag, and brought it to the counter. As I stood there waiting to pay, the cashier started waving her arms and speaking angrily to me in French. I couldn't imagine what she was saying or what the problem was. She kept holding the tomato and shaking it at me. I had made a mistake, but I did not know what to do to correct it. What I did do was leave the tomato at the cashier's counter, pay for the rest of my groceries, and walk out of the grocery store feeling very foolish and very humiliated.

After this experience I could have decided never to buy toma-toes again. By doing so, I would have avoided further stress, but I would not have learned anything. So the next morning I shared with my class what had happened to me the day before. They all laughed at me and explained that I had forgotten to take my tomato over to the scale, where I needed to press the button with the picture of the tomato on it and wait for the machine to spit out a sticker with the correct price. They explained that the sticker had to be on the plastic bag *before* I went to the cashier.

So the next day I went back and selected two tomatoes because I was feeling pretty sure of myself. I put them on the scale, weighed them, and out came the price sticker. When I went to the cashier's counter, the price was on the bag, so there was no problem. However, I was not content to buy just the two tomatoes; I wanted a loaf of French bread too. I picked one up, selected a bag, put the bread in, and carried this to the counter with the tomatoes. The cashier once again waved her arms and yelled at me. Finally, in a huffy sort of way, she rang up my bill, and I paid and went out.

This time I had succeeded in getting out of the store with my purchases, but I was still distressed because I did not under-stand the new problem. Once more I went back to my class and told them my experience. Again they laughed. They explained to me that there were numbers underneath the loaves of bread. A number corresponded to the size bag I should use. The bag, of course, showed the cashier how much to charge me for a particular loaf of bread. Thanks to my class, I was able to reflect on my distressing experiences, gain new information, and then learn how to shop effectively in a Belgian supermarket. Further, the reflection led to some generalizations about the role of the customer and the role of the cashier in European supermarkets, which in turn contributed to my cultural understanding of them.

The notion of processing experiences captures the essence of experiential learning as a methodology for classroom use. A particular course or portion of a course is structured to create the involvement and dissonance that allows reflective learning. We have found these techniques particularly helpful in training workshops on multicultural partnership. We employed several simulation exercises with adult learners from fourteen West African countries in a workshop in Cameroon in 2000. The goal of each simulation was to help these adults understand some of the sources of communication failure in partnerships and then through reflection to find ways to renew their relationships and improve communication. Because these adults expected lectures, we designed a workshop experience that began each day with substantive lectures. When they were mentally tired from listening to lectures, we divided them into small groups for the simulations that created dissonance and that engaged their minds, bodies, and emotions. They then spent more than two hours each day in guided small group discussions, reflecting on their real-life experiences through the lenses of lecture and simulation exercises. The participants in this workshop found the experiential learning exercises to be a catalyst for powerful reflection and application of lecture content to real life.

Strengths and Weaknesses of Experiential Learning

Experiential learning has both strengths and weaknesses. Its focus on experience and emotional responses, rather than on information, makes student preparation and measurement of student learning more subjective. Some people thrive on this kind of learning and find it to be far more interesting and valuable than sitting in a chair and taking notes from a predetermined syllabus or text. Others feel that experiential learning is too fuzzy or messy. They prefer to process a concrete body of information. The group of experiences that constitute the lesson may or may not seem valid to them, and they may resist the essential steps of debriefing, reflecting, and adapting or experimenting with their behavior. The most resistant students dislike situations in which they lack control, are uncertain of the outcome, and might be made to look foolish.

When the subject for a course focuses on interpersonal relationships, it is possible to design an entire course that uses experiential learning. The Korean illustration above was precisely that type of course. Other subjects, such as mathematics or history, are better taught using a variety of techniques. In our workshops in Africa on intercultural partnerships, we designed each day to include morning lectures, at least one experiential learning exercise, and substantive discussion. We found that a team exercise was a far more effective teaching tool than a lecture when dealing with team relationships and led to substantive reflection, discussion, and application.

Teachers who use experiential learning may provide a syllabus but are not afraid to work outside its parameters. In other words, teaching can happen almost spontaneously depending on the teachable moments and the composition of the class. When something happens, either outside or within the class, it becomes a vehicle for teaching a particular concept. Most missionary training programs recognize that experiential learning offers the most hope for helping new recruits understand and appreciate a different culture. If people have only cognitive information, they are unprepared for situations that differ from the text or their understanding of it. The power of experiential learning lies in its unpredictability, its simulation of experiences people are likely to encounter, and the creation of a controlled context for action, reflection, and learning.

I have also used this method in testing. Instead of a written final, students take a performance final, wherein they must in a creative fashion cover all the concepts of the course and present them to me. A colleague who teaches in Africa says he cannot use a performance final because students would be upset. They want the "real" test. So he gives a written final then plans the performance final as a course conclusion and celebration. He says students learn the material much better when they have to figure out how to present it rather than simply write about it, but their anxiety level diminishes when they know the performance does not replace the written test.

Some learners are culturally or emotionally biased against this approach to teaching. Some people are emotionally threatened by these techniques and therefore do not learn well. Rather than growing and changing, they reject the method and sometimes become more entrenched in their outlook and behavior. For whatever cultural or personal reasons, they do not readily connect such experiences with cognitive growth.

A second liability of this approach is the cost of preparation. While it seems like an easy way to teach, I find it much more difficult than lecturing. My preparation for each session takes twice as long and when tested in the classroom may not produce the results I had planned. To create powerful simulations, one must have an intuitive grasp of the connection between abstract concepts and constructed experiences. The instructor must also have a bond with the students and have a sense of the point they are at and how far they might move along a continuum of change. It also helps to be vulnerable, sharing personal failures and successes, and to have a secure sense of personal identity and competence, because often students experiencing dissonance lash out at the instructor in their frustration.

One of the pedagogical benefits of experiential learning is that students must employ intelligences other than the linguistic and the mathematical, which are traditionally the focus of schooling. In fact, people who use only those two intelligences find themselves at a disadvantage in such a format, whereas people who excel at the spatial, the musical, the bodily kinesthetic, or the personal intelligences find they are suddenly able to use abilities they had repressed because they were not valued at school. In addition, experiential learning allows a teacher to observe student reactions to dissonance and thus focus more intentionally on specific character attributes that will ultimately contribute to cross-cultural success or failure.

We do not propose, however, that the experiential approach is the answer to the question of how to help students develop their various intelligences. Academic endeavors *do* demand that a person master a body of knowledge, write a coherent research paper, and be proficient in mathematics to a certain level. The best kind of learning encompasses both the experiential and the cognitive approaches. Each of these provides something different for students, and each reflects the kinds of expectations people have. For example, in the Australian aborigine context mentioned earlier, people learn best by doing. But introducing things such as music, dance, and proverbs into the schooling experience throws people off balance because, they say, that is not school. Schooling has certain kinds of behaviors attached to it, as discussed in chapter 3.

Teaching for Biblical Transformation

Teaching for transformation of character and ministry is the most difficult of all teaching challenges. Seminaries, colleges, and secondary schools excel in the transmission of information, but few take responsibility for the character and performance of their graduates. Most recognize the critical need for character and spiritual formation, but few have found effective ways to achieve these objectives. Those who have been successful have a strong experiential component to their curriculum. In an excellent study of a seminary in the Philippines, Tjoh Dju Ng (2000) demonstrates how faculty members shape the character and ministry of their students through community relationships, accountability, and experiential training for ministry. Following the pattern of Jesus and his disciples described in the Gospels, the professors take students with them to do ministry together, and then they send them out two by two.

In our complex urban societies, where people's work and family commitments consume their lives, the methods described here offer an alternative for those who cannot live and work with a mentor. Using simulations of experience, followed by thoughtful group and personal reflection, teachers can bring students to points of decision and change in their personal lives and ministries. In our two-week workshop with missionaries and national leaders in Cameroon, the simulations and debriefings, more than any other factor, led the participants to confess their judgmental attitudes toward one another and to make commitments to renew the spiritual foundations of their working relationships. They acknowledged that they had been about the work of ministry but had lost the spiritual unity essential for partnership in the work of the kingdom.

Organizations that train people for cross-cultural work recognize one curious thing about experiential learning: While people feel intuitively that they are better prepared, the actual skills and applications are often not transferred until reinforced in subsequent learning experiences. For example, I conduct an eating exercise in my interpersonal adjustment class, because eating is more than simply satisfying hunger; it provides a window into the social relations of a society (Lingenfelter 1992, 179). Who eats with whom? What kinds of food are acceptable? Does one eat with two hands or only one, with chopsticks, a soup spoon, or a fork? The list goes on. In the simulation, I ask the students to sit in groups of six in a circle on the floor. At each place is a napkin-covered dish. In the center of the circle are three spoons and one pair of chopsticks. Three of the dishes contain meat and rice, while three of them contain only rice. The group has two rules: They may eat only with their right hand, and all conversation must include the entire group. Many issues surface in the debriefing session as we discuss the nature of hospitality and the sharing of resources.

One of my students finished this course and had the opportunity to go on a short-term trip to Central Africa immediately afterward. Mealtimes with local people followed the classroom exercise quite closely. However, the student and his friends grabbed more than their share of meat and failed to observe local practice until gently rebuked by an elderly man with whom they were eating. Why didn't the experience the student had had in class transfer to effective observation and adaptation when he was in Africa? Perhaps the answer lies in the familiarity of the experience and the bondage of habit. While one may remember unusual greeting forms or other exotic differences, eating is something that everybody must do for survival. Once engaged in it, one forgets or ignores differences in the quest to make sure he has "enough."

Biblical transformation is not the automatic outcome of the method. More often than not, people fail in their efforts to become 150-percent persons. Transformation is possible only when individuals confess their sins and commit anew to the work of the Holy Spirit in their lives. Learning is done best when the lessons are repeated so frequently that they become habit. Character change happens when the deepest parts of our histories and personalities are touched.

Biblical transformation involves suffering, repentance, commitment, and practice doing what Jesus has commanded. The classroom is the least effective place for this to occur. Students who have learned to survive by copying copious notes, memorizing them, and regurgitating them on tests cannot understand or appreciate different ways of doing things because they do not see the payoff. And when we use experiential methods to confront them with their values and habits, they will still forget a few days after the exercise.

The young missionary who failed his eating test in Africa and suffered a gentle rebuke took his first true step toward biblical transformation. As he changed his behavior over the next three weeks of ministry, he learned what it means to surrender a habit and to consider others better than oneself. The next step in growth is to apply this learning to other habits of life. If he is like most of us, he will act again out of habit and again suffer rebuke. But if he wills to reflect and learn, he will change. Only as he piles up new experiences and reflects on them in the context of his faith will he begin to move beyond his own cultural biases and be transformed into the image of Christ. This is the essence of becoming 150-percent persons.

Research/Reflection Questions

1. Plan a simple experiential exercise in your classroom focused around a concept you are trying to teach. (See Casse 1979; Kohls & Knight 1994; and Seelye 1996 for examples if you cannot think of one yourself.) Be careful, because the planning will be more difficult than you expect. After you debrief the experience with the students, reflect on the experience yourself. Did it go well? How did students react to it? What would have made it better? How did the hidden curriculum expectations of the students enter into the experience?
2. Using what you learned from the first experiential exercise, create a second one. Was it easier the second time? Why or why not?

eight

False Expectations

In the summer of 1996, I visited a college in the Philippines. I was there to observe a literacy class in one of the local languages. The classroom had plywood walls and a tin roof, and wooden louvers covered the screened windows, which opened to one side. Students sat at long tables writing diligently in small note-books, while several small children played at the side of the room, and two dogs roamed around. Because it was raining, the louvers were closed. There was no electricity, so the room was quite dark. A blackboard covered the front wall, and a folding wall barely screened out the noise from the classroom next door. This classroom may seem primitive to western educators, but teaching in the two-thirds world often occurs in less than ideal circumstances. Some people who are used to classrooms with soundproof walls and electricity find it almost impossible to teach in a school like this. They have even more trouble when classes must be held outside under a tree or in a thatched-roof building with no walls and a dirt floor.

In earlier chapters, we encouraged teachers to prepare men-tally for differences in the ways students think or learn. How-ever, we recognize that some who have prepared for hidden curriculum issues may be derailed by economic and social constraints that do not allow for textbooks, paper, copiers, and other cultural comforts associated with teaching. Some who expect these essentials, which we take for granted, may have a rude awakening. False expectations cause more stress when teaching cross-culturally than any other factor. This chapter explores several of these false expectations and suggests ways to respond as Christians committed to incarnational teaching.

False Expectations about Resources

In some places, a teacher's desk or chalk or chairs cannot be taken for granted. For example, I observed a university class in a relatively new facility in Africa. When the professor walked in, he discovered he did not have a desk. A student quickly turned a student desk around so the professor could place his notes on something, and the professor accepted the improvisation and began to teach. Pamela George (1995) relates stories of teachers who did not accept the absence of a desk or a lectern as gracefully. Instead, they confronted their hosts, expressing their frustrations about having little or no office space, inadequate textbooks from which to teach, and no technical support.

The political and economic challenges of a developing country are illustrated by a colleague's experiences during a Fulbright semester in Turkmenistan. She was training English as a Foreign Language teachers and could not locate a copier either at the university or at a public place in the capital city to reproduce class materials. Through her Fulbright connections, she gained minimal access to a copier at a related agency, but the paper supplies ran out about a third of the way through her semester there. To conserve paper, she designed exercises using a quarter of a piece of $8\frac{1}{2}$-by-11-inch paper. To make matters more difficult, university administrators canceled classes at a moment's notice for reasons not explained to her, and often a class of twelve students would have only two or three in attendance. Fortunately, she had prepared herself mentally for these frustrations, having taught English in other countries. Most westerners are not prepared, however, and they panic when circumstances require changes in class management or the adaptation of course content.

Western dependence on increasingly sophisticated technology has hampered our ability to be creative in the classroom. A friend who teaches at a university in Thailand relates that when she returned to the United States and asked for advice on how to teach, her colleagues told her to put her lectures on Power-Point, a computer software program that is used in many American university classrooms. When she pointed out that she could not count on reliable electricity at the university, thus restricting her use of a computer, her colleagues did not have any other suggestions to offer.

Low Technology: An Incarnational Response

In the United States, one of the most popular replies to allegations that schools are not effective is that teachers do not have enough money to obtain the necessary equipment and supplies. When a school has problems, leaders often demand more money and trust technology to solve the problems. Working in the two-thirds world, where resources are limited, teachers need to have a "tool kit" of ideas that do not rely on expensive technologies but on easily obtainable materials. Students who learn in a holistic fashion or who struggle with the language of instruction need a detailed outline to follow so they can feel comfortable with what the teacher is presenting. If paper and copiers exist, the teacher can hand out the day's material. If these items are luxuries, then the teacher must depend on the blackboard (and hope for chalk!). My colleague who went to Turkmenistan packed a separate box of teaching materials to take along. However, the box never arrived with her luggage. Undismayed, she fell back on plan B—the newsprint in which she had packed some belongings that she smoothed out with an iron. Because she was prepared for things to go wrong, she was able to adapt to the existing cultural context with only a minimum of frustration.

One useful technique to use when materials are limited is called the narrative approach to pedagogy. We hesitate to trumpet it as a "new" method; Africans have used it for years! This technique employs stories to teach ideas and abstract concepts.

A Kenyan student says that one can know truth only as it is embedded in a story, because how else can one recognize abstract concepts? However, most western teachers believe that storytelling is for children or an activity associated with sitting around campfires during a retreat in the mountains. In other words, stories are meant to entertain, not to instruct. Abraham Lincoln frequently used stories to answer questions. He incensed many of his colleagues because they wanted a "straight" answer. Yet in contexts in which confrontation is dealt with indirectly, the story may be the most effective instructional device. (See Steffen 1996 and Elmer 1993 for further discussion of this.)

How could one use this method effectively in a classroom? A teacher or a student might take the role of a particular person and stay in that role for the duration of the class. The Bible provides rich resource material for use, offering characters and situations that speak to many contemporary issues. The tendency in Bible schools is to lecture about the characters and the stories, but only rarely are students invited to be the characters in a story. Western teachers tend to concentrate on the abstract truth embedded in a story, missing the fact that the abstract truth has a context and involves characters who interact with one another and with God. It would be more powerful to *be* Joseph than to talk about Joseph. Character traits, economics, and history come alive when taught in a blend of narrative and reflective dialogue. The Bible includes male and female characters: Abraham's wife, Sarah, for example, has a riveting story to tell, as do Rebekah, Leah, and others. Narrative as a pedagogical method communicates well and does not cost any money to use.

A method that Robert Serpell (1993) found useful in an African context was participatory drama. He records the use of this indigenous theatrical form to discuss life journeys of rural Zambians. Several people developed a story line that followed a group of characters through significant events in their lives. After they told the story, they invited the audience to join in by relating to characters who paralleled their own experiences. Serpell does pose one caution: Before using an indigenous form, be sure you understand its commonly understood meanings. Otherwise, you may communicate something antithetical to what you planned.

Another teaching technique that has been rejected in the western tradition is the memorization of large quantities of material. If one has only a blackboard and copybooks, students can copy material and memorize it. It is helpful to begin with meaningful chunks of text, such as stories, poems, or songs. Many years ago I sat at a Yapese funeral, an event that went on for days, with a five-year-old girl from a family I knew well. I began asking her about her relatives and was amazed that she remembered all the names, the chronologies, and their relationships to her. She had learned these details because they had meaning for her parents and the members in her family as they fulfilled their obligations to one another. In a Bible school or seminary context, students may memorize Bible verses or passages as part of a course. However, when an Indian student told me that he had just finished memorizing the Book of Hebrews and was moving on to Luke, I realized that we often do not provide enough challenge to students trained in the oral tradition, as my five-year-old friend was.

An Indonesian friend (Marantika 2002) who was looking for indigenous techniques to use to teach biblical concepts decided to use *machapat*, a Javanese song form that is narrative in scope. Each song is a story, and each story has a moral principle. She assembled a team of people to put the entire Book of Matthew into this song format so that illiterate villagers could learn the book. Her strategy recognized that Javanese have traditionally rewarded the musical intelligence, and she built on this ready-made opportunity to teach the Bible. The one caveat was that she had to make sure that putting the Word into song did not distort its theological accuracy. The pastors, therefore, worked long and hard to make sure the message was communicated accurately in the musical form.

In colleges and seminaries around the world, teachers and pastors are trained in methods that communicate well in some contexts and poorly in others. They are usually trained in linear, abstract thinking and do not consider visual techniques that will help students whose primary mode of learning is visual and holistic. If they have used visual techniques at all, they have used films or videos, which are powerful but encourage passivity in students. A simple deck of playing cards can illustrate many different things, as can a piece of rope, a ball, or other easily obtainable materials. For example, in a course dealing with opposing views on a subject, one could divide the class into two sides and use a ball to illustrate the arguments raised on both sides of the issue. The possibilities are limited only by the imagination of the teacher.

False Expectations about Curriculum

Every teacher brings to the classroom expectations about curriculum that are rooted in his or her training and experience. When asked to teach, we assume that the subject matter will be the same as that which we have learned and taught. We bring along our materials, our prepackaged lesson plans, and take our place in the classroom. We are the experts, and we assume our knowledge base is right for our assignment. In many situations, nothing could be farther from the truth. Until we understand what our students have already learned and what they will do with what they learn from us, we very likely do not have the "right" material for our assignment.

Curriculum is one of the biggest blind spots faced by expatriate teachers. Stories abound of western seminary professors who assume that arguments for the existence of God or debates about Calvinism vs. Arminianism are the most important theological components of a course, while they ignore issues about the spirit world or how God can have power over illness. Yet the Bible deals with these latter issues in far greater detail than it does with the former. Paul Hiebert (1982) and others have written extensively about the western dichotomistic outlook that separates the natural and the supernatural and omits the "middle"—the world inhabited by spirits. This bias blinds western teachers to the diverse issues addressed in the Bible and often leads them to impose a conceptual structure on Scripture where one does not necessarily exist.

In recent years, a number of authors (e.g., Dyrness 1990; Taylor 2000) have sought to address theological issues from a two-thirds world perspective, and no expatriate should teach theology without learning from and incorporating the insights from such books. William Dyrness (1990), for example, encourages westerners to "listen in on the conversations of theological scholars around the world" (1). Time spent listening to learners will also vastly improve our capacity to design a curriculum that truly serves their needs, regardless of the subject being taught.

False Expectations about Testing

Cultural conflicts over values and behavior concerning testing can be disconcerting to western educators. In the United States, a student studies a specific body of material then takes a test on it to see how much he or she has learned. Several concepts in the preceding sentence demand explication. What does it mean to "study" material, "take a test," and "learn" the material? Is memorizing a body of material the same as studying it? Should tests be taken individually or as a group? Can one consider the material "learned" if the resulting change in behavior (to use Ernest Hilgard and Gordon Bower's 1981 definition) does not occur until several years later? And what does it mean to cheat on a test?

Many teachers express deep frustration about students who cheat on tests. One expatriate teacher working in Ghana relates that she would give a literacy test to one group in the morning then see those students at lunchtime giving all the answers to the afternoon class. To solve this problem, she gave two different tests. However, she adopted a level-1 solution to a level-2 problem. She never asked the question, What is cheating? Educator Ted Ward told me a story of an experience he had in Ghana. When he observed people giving one another answers, he asked for the definition of cheating. One man stood up straight and announced, "Sir, cheating is withholding information from those who need it!" Such a definition is diametrically opposed to the typical western definition and has different consequences. Jerry Harvey (1988), in a lively book he wrote on management principles in the United States, passionately argues that we need to rethink our emphasis on individual work and do much more group learning and testing in order to take advantage of the skills and expertise that each member of a group brings to a problem.

In cross-cultural contexts, teachers will be more effective if they rethink the understandings they bring to the learning and testing process. What is the purpose of a test? Should it be written or oral? In the United States, we rely almost exclusively on written tests, yet in Europe, most graduate examinations are oral, a concept foreign to Americans.

Written exams often require students to repeat information given by the professor word for word. In many two-thirds world countries, a national ministry of education produces examinations that all students must take at various points in their schooling. Passing these exams is extremely important, as they offer a ticket to the university. Teachers "teach to the test," and thus the emphasis is on learning the information necessary to proceed to the next level. Introducing high-level questions such as What is the story's moral? or How would you synthesize the authors' conflicting arguments? often leads to confusion. Students prefer the lower domain of facts because facts are easier to memorize and repeat back to the teacher.

The cross-cultural teacher, therefore, must grapple with complex cultural realities. Students may value group learning and try to support one another in the testing process. Under some circumstances, that may be the most effective method to achieve learning. The culture of schooling may lead students to expect tests that follow a certain predictable pattern, and if they do not, the teacher has violated a cultural norm. When students live in a nation in which national exams are the norm, they must learn how to prepare for and take these exams. The best teachers will develop multiple strategies to evaluate student progress and enable them to learn.

False Expectations about Visual Learning

"A picture is worth a thousand words," but pictures do not always transmit their meanings across cultures as neatly as we would like. In fact, sometimes they hinder and distort rather than clarify and illuminate a point or concept. SIL, a Bible translation mission organization that focuses on literacy in order to teach people to read the Bible once it is translated, has worked extensively with nonliterates on many such cross-cultural issues. They have learned that often pictures communicate something entirely different from what was intended. An SIL colleague who works in Brazil says that if one wants to illustrate the word *jaguar* for the Kayapo, an Indian tribe, the animal must be drawn from the front, as that is the direction from which Kayapo men see the animal when they shoot.

In chapter 1, I related the story of my disastrous attempt to teach Yapese children color categories through visual aids, which I mistakenly thought were universal. Since that time, through experience and the work of such people as Brent Berlin and Paul Kay (1969) and Peter Farb (1988), I have learned that while all human beings have the same biological capabilities of seeing, culture determines which things are actually "seen." My experience with the colors blue and green on Yap illustrated this. If I had known better, I would have asked the students to tell me the names they used for these colors. But even if I had done so, the visuals would still have been inadequate because a picture of a palm tree cannot convey all the possible variations of color that a real one can.

Jon Arensen, an SIL colleague who worked among the Murle in the barren mud flats and savannas of Sudan, tried a similar experiment with color categories and had similar results. He learned that the Murle have several hundred words for the color brown, but they have only one word for both blue and green. Further, when he tried eliciting the specific words by using slides of the colors, the Murle got impatient with him. They told him he had to touch a cow's hide or see the differences between wet and dry to name a color properly.

The following guidelines will help a western educator evaluate the potential utility of pictures. First, pictures communicate best when the subjects are familiar. Second, if you are drawing the pictures, do not include too much detail. For example, concentrate on human activity, not on tufts of grass or clouds. Third, make sure the details in the pictures are accurate. Finally, the presentations should be straightforward, because often people do not follow a sequence of pictures and reach the conclusions we intended.

An anthropological story (Werner and Bower 1982, 12–14) that has appeared in many texts tells of the health worker who wanted to teach people about the dangers of the malaria-carrying mosquito and how a simple mosquito net would be a most effective deterrent. He made a mock-up of a mosquito large enough so that people could see what he was illustrating. Several months later he returned to the village and discovered that people had not been using mosquito nets at all. When he questioned them, one villager replied, "Oh, we don't have mosquitoes as big as the one you showed us, so we don't need nets." The attempt backfired simply because the details were not accurate.

False Expectations about Status

The culture of prestige often surprises foreign teachers. In some places in Asia, students stand and either bow or clap when the teacher enters the classroom. Some western teachers comment on how uncomfortable this makes them feel, and one person told me that she vigorously discouraged this practice in her classes. What she did not realize was that she was breaking down respect patterns concerning the ascribed status of a teacher. The consequences of such a seemingly innocuous decision may not surface until many years later.

In some cultural settings, age and gender are essential factors in one's social standing. A twenty-four-year-old Anglo female teacher, no matter how many degrees she has, because of her gender and age may not be granted the status she expects as a qualified teacher. For Americans, this causes much misunderstanding. Women who already feel they must work twice as hard as men find that they face an impenetrable wall with regard to professional status.

Still another cultural surprise may be appropriate dress. In America, the current trend in businesses and churches is casual dress. The expectations in a status-oriented society, however, demand that a teacher dress according to his or her position. Many Americans cringe at the thought of wearing a coat and tie or high heels and stockings, but if that is the accepted dress, then the western educator should follow. One American I met in Africa told me that he had asked his African colleagues if it were okay for him to dress casually, and they had said it was. However, not one of them dressed that way, which should have been a clue that they were being polite rather than giving him a straight answer. Western educators teaching in major cities around the world will find that their colleagues have specific expectations about appropriate dress for teachers. Another example comes from a Chinese colleague who reported that dangling earrings prove extremely distracting to students. People working in rural contexts will no doubt encounter a different set of rules. Whatever the context, find out what is expected.

In my (Sherwood's) work with Marvin K. Mayers, *Ministering Cross-Culturally* (1986), we explain this conflict about dress in terms of values about personal prestige. People for whom prestige is achieved know that they have worked hard for their degrees and feel that people should accept them on the basis of performance, not external factors such as dress. However, people who believe that prestige is ascribed insist that one obey the implicit rules that go along with the position. If you are a professor in this latter context, you dress formally in accord with the cultural standard. Respect comes with the position, but one must still act according to the rules.

False Expectations about Planning

In western schools, there is a strongly developed culture of planning. This value is so important that accreditors may censure school leaders who fail to maintain adequate systems of planning. In this cultural climate, most teachers and school administrators develop habits and expectations for planning in their daily and long-term routines. We plan budgets, maintain an inventory of materials and supplies, schedule maintenance, and conduct periodic evaluations to revise programs and plan for the future.

Western teachers who work under national leaders in two-thirds world schools frequently fault these leaders for failing to meet their planning expectations. Mayers and I (Sherwood) (1986) characterized these differences as a crisis and noncrisis value dichotomy. The western teacher who expects planning may be crisis-oriented, while the national leaders may be noncrisis oriented.

Crisis people plan for the future, needing to know where they are going and what steps will get them there. They like goals and objectives because these provide the incentives to plan ahead. Noncrisis people tend to take things as they come, and when surprises arise, they simply adjust accordingly. Nothing frustrates a crisis-oriented western educator more than running out of paper because someone forgot to order it ahead of time or not having the appropriate textbooks when classes begin.

A noncrisis orientation prevails throughout much of the two-thirds world, not because all non-westerners think this way but because economic and political uncertainties force such people to accept ambiguity and unforeseen events. One may order all the supplies necessary for the coming school year well ahead of time, but if tribal war stops the planes from flying or the trucks from driving, the materials will not arrive on time. Therefore, most people find that a noncrisis attitude helps them adapt to these unknowns with less discomfort and frustration.

Coping with False Expectations

The teaching realities described in this chapter represent only a few of the many issues a western teacher is likely to encounter. We chose to emphasize these because they illustrate potential problems likely to crop up in various cultural contexts. Throughout the book we have emphasized the importance of beginning as a learner, seeking to understand the people with whom we work, and adding new alternatives to our repertoire of strategies for teaching and maintaining relationships. While we are inspired by the vision to become 150-percent persons, we must also understand who we are and accept our strengths as the place to begin our response.

For example, with reference to planning, some western educators may describe themselves as noncrisis and are not bothered by what crisis people refer to as a lack of planning. Of course, these same noncrisis people tend to be more inefficient in situations in which efficiency would resolve many problems. If, on the other hand, you are a crisis-oriented person, you can prepare for work in a developing country by imagining various scenarios in your mind. A colleague in Turkmenistan is a crisis-oriented person. Yet she has trained herself to work in noncrisis contexts by expecting that things won't work and allowing for various responses. If plan A does not work (e.g., the box of materials is lost), then she has a plan B and possibly a plan C already in mind. Sometimes none of her plans work, and that is when her commitment to find new cultural options relieves her potential frustration. An African skill of "strategic waiting" may prove much more effective than "strategic planning" (Ouedraogo and Hill 2002, 14). If she reacts negatively and angers those around her, she might as well return home, because trust once destroyed is more difficult to rebuild.

Whatever the issue, curriculum, testing, or status as a teacher, we bring unique and valued strengths to the people with whom we work. They appreciate our presence and look with anticipation for our contribution. When we experience the blows of failed expectations, we need to remember that the people around us are probably trying to help in ways they best understand.

As you become a 150-percent person, you will think less about what you must give up and more about what you can add to your options and capabilities. The people around you have a full range of strategies for effective teaching and working relationships that they are usually quite willing to teach you. Your best resource is to apply the simple instructions of Jesus in Matthew 7:1–12. First, do not be quick to judge and condemn, and do not assume you understand why something is happening to you. Rather, apply the fundamental principles of a loving relationship—ask, seek, and knock. Find the people you think are responsible for your frustration and explain that you do not understand what is happening. Then ask what they are trying to do and how they are trying to serve you. Seek to understand their views concerning what is happening and why. And keep on knocking until the door of relationship is open and you have understanding that relieves your mutual pain and empowers you and them to work more effectively together.

Research/Reflection Questions

1. In the two value pairs discussed in this chapter, status achieved or ascribed and crisis or noncrisis, which ones describe you? How flexible are you? Do you need order and structure in your life? Do you have a difficult time getting things done on a schedule?

2. Learn about different cultural perceptions, such as color categories and illustrations, by talking with students from other language backgrounds. Several years ago in a Christian university, a Korean student was graded harshly in her student teaching because she told the students in her class the sun was red, and the Anglo supervising teacher insisted it was orange. Yet all over Asia, including the Japanese flag and the logo for Korean Airlines, the sun is clearly depicted as being red.

nine

Learning to Teach
Cross-Culturally

The war in Liberia raged for weeks around African Bible College. Finally, the situation was so serious that Del sent Becky and the other women and children to the Ivory Coast, where they would be safe. He and a few of his African faculty colleagues stayed with the students to protect the school. Del had invested deeply in these students, loving them, learning their culture, and becoming a patron to many. He knew the Liberian soldiers had destroyed schools and mission compounds in Monrovia, and he dreaded the thought of letting the college fall into their hands. He had built relationships with some of the local officials, visiting them in their offices, homes, and even the hospital. Every other week Del provided the military leaders with a bag of rice, and when soldiers came to the school, he welcomed them and extended hospitality as he would to friends. They, in turn, provided the school much needed security.

In spite of the fighting around them, the students asked Del to keep teaching. They were eager to learn and wanted to finish the year of study if at all possible. The systematic bombing by

Nigeria from Monrovia northward, city by city, continued. As the bombing drew closer to their city of Yekepa, Del and the students dug bomb shelters and hid their vehicles under tree branches. It was not until the Nigerian jet bombers flew low over the campus and the community that many of the students and many in the community were ready to evacuate. Taking his cue from most of the students and people in the community, Del traveled to the Ivory Coast.

A year later, during a cease-fire, they were able to return to the community and finish the academic year. Graduation was a historic occasion. In spite of war in parts of the country, military rule in the community, and UN peacekeepers on patrol, Del and his colleagues at African Bible College presented bachelor's degrees to many graduates.

Because Del began as a learner, the students and the school carried on under impossible circumstances. The school survived the first years of war and graduated a class of students who would not have finished without Del's commitment. While Del worked hard to have a quality school, its success was not due to exceptional technology, facilities, and teaching. Del and Becky studied the expectations of their students, learned patterns of relationship in their cultures, and adapted their methods and expectations to the worldviews of their students.

The preceding chapters have tried to illuminate some of the cultural differences that challenge western teachers in a nonwestern context. The goal has been to help teachers become 150-percent persons, learning how to use the existing cultural patterns of teaching and student learning to develop effective methods for teaching cross-culturally. We recognize that our suggestions for cultural learning only begin to tap the depth of knowledge and practice of a given culture. Every culture is complex, and it may take years for teachers to learn how to live and work in ways that approximate the expertise of those who learn the culture as children.

This chapter presents some additional tools that will help teachers learn about the culture beyond the classroom and connect with people who can help them participate, like Del and Becky, in a wider community of relationships. Some can be used before arriving on the scene; others may stimulate new avenues of daily learning in the community. The best teachers continue to learn about the people they seek to serve and from that understanding become competent participants in the local community.

The Political Context of Schooling

In the true story of Del and Becky in Liberia, understanding the political context of African Bible College was critical to their survival. Del spent hours building relationships with government officials and army officers. He participated in community functions, made the school's facilities available to the community for functions, sat on community boards, and distributed relief supplies. His involvement opened up a floodgate of opportunities to influence community policy, and the community became a security shield for the school during threatening situations. Del also kept abreast of the shifts in power among military factions in Liberia. He tried to maintain a neutral position for the school and to extend hospitality to officials who came to the school. While their situation of crisis was hopefully unique, teachers never teach in a vacuum! It is absolutely essential to have a basic understanding of the political context in which a school operates.

The best way to begin is to find the most current books on the political and economic situations of the country. These works usually provide the important historical context of the nation and an interpretive analysis that helps one process complex information and draw applications for working in that nation. To review more current events, read news sources on the Internet and find articles that provide analysis of these events.

When you arrive in the country, get to know the officials who have authority over you. Begin with the local officials in your school and community, visiting them periodically and assuring them of your support. If the situation permits, seek to meet higher government officials to signal your respect and appreciation for the opportunity to teach in their schools. Del and Becky intentionally placed themselves in a vulnerable position, giving resources to others when they hardly had enough, so that reciprocity could occur and deeper relationships could be formed.

A British literacy worker related how she took the first primers in an African local language to the minister of education so he could see what she was doing. As it happened, the minister was from the language group with whom she was working. He was so excited about the literacy project that he offered to write one of the more advanced primers in the series. It turned out to be a very fruitful partnership, all because she had not excluded the national education department from the process of teaching adults how to read.

We cannot overemphasize the importance of learning about the political realities while you are a beginning learner. One of our students conducted research in the Ukraine a few years after the collapse of communism. He discovered that asking seemingly innocuous questions such as "How many students are in the school?" produced a great deal of suspicion. Why did he want to know? What was he going to do with the information? Further, when he tried to observe classes or ask for advice on teaching, he found people extremely reluctant to help. He soon learned that these activities were considered politically risky; people were afraid he might disclose information that could cost them their jobs or their standing with officials. He had to develop other nonthreatening ways of learning to continue his research program.

Del and Becky provide a model of how to understand a political context and be incarnational teachers. They followed the commands of Scripture to respect and submit to those in authority (1 Peter 2:13) and worked to build relationships with haughty and sometimes impetuous officials. When the war threatened to engulf them and the school, their relationships stood as a wall of protection for nearly three years until the country fell and they had to abandon the school to protect the students.

When we internalize the principles of Scripture to respect everyone with whom we work (1 Peter 2:17), to submit to those who govern our work (1 Peter 2:13), and to do good things for those around us (1 Peter 2:15), we create an environment of peace and goodwill that will be a blessing to others. When we work as guests in a foreign country, these actions are especially important, because our most meaningful witness is how we treat the officials, administrators, teachers, and students we serve.

Creating a Place in Community

To begin to feel at home in another cultural setting, you must develop the same kinds of relationships and friendships that you have in your home community. Most American Christians have three significant spheres of relationship: family, workplace, and church. After many years of consulting in mission field settings, we have found that missionaries tend to turn their mission community into all three. This is disastrous for those who envision a ministry that touches the lives of people in the local community and culture. What can you do to avoid this retreat from the people and local community in which you serve?

First, learn to know many, if not all, of the families of the national coworkers in your workplace. If you are working in a school with national teachers, visit your national colleagues in their homes. If most of the other teachers are outsiders like you, then visit the families of your students and of the staff working in the school. Don't wait for an invitation! Often the most acceptable form of visiting is "dropping in." If you are not sure about local customs governing visiting, ask a colleague. Also ask people how they make new friends.

Plan ahead of time how to make each visit a learning experience. Take notes, writing down the names of children and other family members. Ask your colleagues to tell you how they became teachers at the school. Invite them to tell you about their families and relatives in the local community. When you get home, make notes in a journal about the visit. Write down things you want to remember about the people and the family and whether they gave you a gift or food so that you know how to reciprocate when they visit you. You could even make a map of the town in which you are living, locating each of the families of your fellow workers or students on the map. This will give you a greater appreciation for the distances they must travel and their family situations.

The second important step is building a support network to help you meet your daily needs. Wherever you live, you will find local shops that supply food, supplies, and services for people in the community. Plan a walking tour of the services nearby. Stop at a shop and introduce yourself. Ask the people in the shop to tell you their names, and take time to talk with them. Tell them you are a teacher working in their community, and ask them for help in finding the things you need. If you cannot speak their language, this is a good time to begin learning, so you can communicate better with the people around you. While you may find cheaper goods at larger stores farther away, local relationships are of greater value than the money you may save by driving elsewhere.

As you survey the neighborhood, select those people and places that seem to best serve your needs, and plan second and third visits. It is always useful in your follow-up visits to ask the simple question, "How do people make friends here?" The question signals that you are interested in friendship, and the answers will help you understand the expectations of those around you. Listen to their answers, and make notes in your journal to help you plan strategies for building your network.

In the normal course of our lives, we need a variety of support services. Mechanics, carpenters, electricians, and other service workers are helpful in times of crisis. Making an effort to get acquainted before you need them can prove helpful. Giving small gifts is often a way to begin relationships. A staff secretary in Cameroon periodically placed a bar of chocolate in the post office box just to ensure that the mail kept coming. These small, thoughtful acts lead to relationships that bring ready help in times of crisis.

Finding Family and Fellowship

The third step for integration into a local community is to identify a local family and a local church that will become your family and church away from home. Through the process of visiting your colleagues, you may find two or three families with whom you and your family feel most comfortable. You may want to explore deeper relationships with these people. A second visit signals a desire for a continuing relationship. In second and third visits, plan to share stories of your family and background, and invite your hosts to share their stories. Talking about your different experiences of marriage, parent/child relationships, and family obligations helps each of you understand the mysterious background of the other. The conversations will be interesting but also helpful in building cross-cultural understanding within both families.

In many two-thirds world cultures, a deep relationship does not begin until there is debt and reciprocal obligation. We have found that one of the best ways to signal our desire for a deeper relationship is to ask others for help. This phase of the relationship causes much stress to many westerners. For self-sufficient westerners, asking for help is much more difficult than giving it, yet asking is the most important step in initiating relationships in many non-western cultural contexts. By committing yourself to receive and to give, you signal a desire for a deep, supportive relationship. If you are proactive in visiting several local families, you will have a much better chance of developing commitments with a local family whom you will enjoy as your family away from home.

Sometimes people will visit you, and some will ask you for help. Usually such visits and requests are invitations to develop deeper relationships. While you can and should show hospitality, you cannot and should not accept all invitations for relationship. Ask your national colleagues for advice on how to respond to those who come to your door and make requests.

Choosing a family away from home can be fraught with difficulty. You may explore a relationship with one family and find that their expectations are more than you can sustain. That is why you need to network with two or more families for a time before you invest deeply in one. During our time on Yap, we developed deep relationships with two families, one in the village in which we lived and the other in a community ten miles away. Each family was important to us, providing support for our needs and requiring giving on our part for holidays and other family events.

Choosing a church is often much more difficult than choosing a family. Most Christians have deep emotional and spiritual feelings about worship that are inextricably woven together with language and culture. Attending services in another language can be boring and emotionally and spiritually empty. As a consequence, teachers who do not speak local languages gravitate to English-language services attended by other expatriates. While this helps them meet their needs for emotional and spiritual nurture, it disconnects them from the local community of believers.

One way out of this problem is to redefine involvement in church from "attending services" to "sharing in ministry." In most contexts, there are many ways to share in the ministry of a community of believers. Begin by asking your fellow teachers about the various ministries of their churches. Ask which of those ministries you might get involved in with your limited language ability. Try two or three until you find a small group of people and a ministry that fits you and the members of your family.

Once you connect with a few families in the church, visit each family with the purpose of spiritual fellowship. Tell them about your conversion and spiritual journey, and ask them to tell you their stories. Share songs that have special meaning for you. Learn about one another's spiritual gifts, and encourage one another by recounting how God has blessed you when exercising these gifts. Comfort one another in times of sickness and sorrow. Minister to others together and to one another as you have family needs.

Once you have found deep spiritual relationships with a few families, you may find that while the services are still intellectually unsatisfying, the relationships and mutual ministry are very satisfying. You may still choose to attend an English service for spiritual and cultural refreshment. Yet you have connected with a local community of believers for ministry.

We cannot emphasize enough the importance of learning the local language. Anyone who truly desires to learn the culture of the students he or she is teaching must commit to learning their language. In some multicultural contexts, this will be impossible. When students in the same school come from different ethnic groups and have different languages, the school language may be the only one they have in common. At minimum a western teacher should work to learn the national language of the country in which the school is located. In the process of learning the language, the culturally sensitive western teacher can ask questions that will aid his or her understanding of the ways in which institutions work and people relate to one another. Tom and Elizabeth Brewster have developed an excellent set of tools called *Language Acquisition Made Practical* (1976) that will guide you in this learning process.

Coping with Culture Shock

Becoming a 150-percent person is never easy. In fact, the process is often painful and accompanied by stress. Sometimes the stress is so great that in spite of our best intentions and efforts, we suffer periods of discouragement and even depression. Culture shock is an emotional state of stress, depression, and varying degrees of impaired function caused by constant exposure to people whose way of life conflicts with our own. Culture shock is a normal state of affairs for anyone who spends six months or more living and working in another culture. Some people experience shock for a short period of time, while for others it lasts much longer. Some have severe reactions, while others have mild reactions. For some the condition is chronic, and for others recovery can be rapid and complete. Teachers are not exempt. Therefore, we conclude this book with a discussion of the common stages of culture adjustment (see table 9.1) and steps for coping with this state of distress.

According to Kalvero Oberg (1960), many teachers intially experience a honeymoon or a tourist reaction to living and working cross-culturally. In the rush of making the decisions necessary to uproot self and/or family, the westerner thinks first of the tangible things: What should we take, and what will be available for purchase in the country of destination? Friends may bombard us with articles or personal anecdotes about their cross-cultural experiences, and by the time the packing and the good-byes are behind us, we are both excited and fearful. Like tourists, we find the first few weeks filled with exotic experiences! The unusual foods, the noisy street markets packed with bargains, the smiling children, the nice guest homes/hotels, and the fear of being robbed on the street overwhelm us with sensations of both delight and uncertainty.

The second stress stage begins when one tries to settle in and live on a daily basis in a new place. Getting a phone may be a six-month trial of patience (if you can get one at all). Electricity may be sporadic, and you may lose all your computer data

Table 9.1

Stages of Adjustment

Honeymoon or tourist
Culture stress
Culture shock
Adjustment
Reentry: Difficulty accepting home culture

Table 9.2

Types of Responses to Culture Shock

Dysfunctional Responses

Flight
Severe withdrawal
Aggressiveness
Dependence

Functional Responses

Make the nationals your teachers
Reflection and/or prayer
Gratitude and graciousness
Assertiveness
Flexibility

(Adapted from Oberg 1960, 177–82)

when the power fails. The books you assumed had been ordered for the courses you will be teaching have not arrived (and you suspect they have not even been ordered). We all deal with stress, but what sets this stress apart from that encountered in our own culture is the ineffectiveness of our normal coping strategies. We try home-culture responses (level-1 solutions) to new-culture problems, and they do not work. For example, complaining to the telephone company may produce many polite apologies but no phone, no matter how much one threatens or cajoles. We do not have the right information to solve the problems.

Stage three, culture shock, occurs when the stresses mount and overwhelm a person. People cope with shock in different ways. Oberg suggests that people devise functional and dysfunctional responses (see table 9.2). One dysfunctional response to culture shock is to decide to go home. The stresses become so painful that a person just wants to quit. Sometimes this reaction may be the appropriate one. However, at this phase of cultural learning, when so much is still new, very few people are capable of devising culturally appropriate solutions (level-2 learning) to their problems.

A second response may be to withdraw almost completely. Withdrawal, a psychological response, often leads to depression, which may in turn lead to physical problems. Some who withdraw may cope by building a world that resembles the one they left, and they survive with marginal success for limited periods of time. It is easy to criticize colonial or missionary compounds, but they represent home-culture solutions (level-1) to host-culture problems (level-2) that some people are unable to solve.

A third response is to be tough and confront in order to survive, especially if this is a cultural strategy that has worked in the past. A Russian visitor to Southern California had this experience in a discount store. When the clerk did not do what he asked, he yelled at him and made quite a scene. My friend Joe, who was with him, recognized this as a strategy used in Russia, where Joe had once worked. But the aggressiveness backfired, even in confrontational America, and the Russian was nearly escorted out of the store by security guards.

In the last dysfunctional response, dependence, the outsider stops making an attempt to understand or negotiate differences and simply does whatever someone tells him or her to do. This response is also called "going native." I watched my daughter adopt this pattern of adjustment as she attempted to cope with Yapese culture at age three. She refused to speak English, she wore only Yapese clothes, and she did whatever the others did.

There are several functional responses to culture shock that offer hope. First, you can make the nationals your teachers. This involves risk, because sometimes they may deliberately mislead you. If you do not reach out and trust someone from a different culture, however, you will never experience the level of learning you need to survive.

Oberg cites withdrawal as a functional response, but we prefer to label the process "reflection and/or prayer." We have included prayer in this reflective component because one must acknowledge one's limitations and have a sense of peace about situations that are out of one's control.

Another response that contributes to adjustment is gratitude and graciousness. When one is gracious about accepting a cup of hot tea when one would prefer a cold drink of water, the act goes a long way in helping others see you as accepting of their hospitality. Being grateful for a mosquito net instead of complaining about a lack of air-conditioning is another example. In 1 Thessalonians 5:18, Paul encourages believers to "give thanks in all circumstances." The act of giving thanks helps a person take small steps toward contentment, regardless of his or her environment or situation.

Assertiveness is another functional response. In some situations, retaining a personal identity commitment may help you to let go of other cultural values that are less important to your personal survival. For example, a missionary might refuse to drink alcohol when local people drink to excess but accept their invitation to chew betel nut, a mild stimulant. One does not have to lose one's cultural identity or do things exactly as another does them in order to adjust. As Casse (1979, 88) says, "I am OK and you are OK."

The final functional response to culture shock is flexibility. Flexibility is a cultivated habit for 150-percent persons. They choose options from different cultures based on the context. In a western context, they play by western rules, and in a local context, they play by local rules. They understand that status is both achieved and ascribed, and they know when each is important. They know how to plan for effective teaching and how to wait when plans do not work. They are at ease working with ample or limited economic resources and materials. They enjoy local food and hospitality and rejoice in something special from home. Having become detached from many of the certainties of their home culture and having embraced many of the options of the host culture, they enjoy a freedom from the tyrannies of each.

If we successfully cope with culture shock and learn to live in and enjoy a new culture, we face one more adjustment hurdle: returning home! Reentry into a past world may be as difficult as adapting to a new one. After we have seen how differently people order their lives, it is difficult to return home and accept the culture we left. We find ourselves critical and wonder how

friends and family can be so preoccupied with material posses-
sions or sports and so disinterested in what we experienced.
Suddenly, we find it more difficult to accept our home culture
than it was to accept one that initially seemed so strange and
later became so comfortable.

Marvin K. Mayers (1987) writes that acceptance of self is the
beginning of change. This takes on an even greater urgency for
a western teacher heading to a two-thirds world country to teach.
You cannot change your past, and this past, your cultural and
emotional prison, has conditioned you to react in specific ways.
For example, if you are easily angered by perceived incompetence, this trait will be exacerbated in a cross-cultural setting.
You will perceive incompetence every time things are not done
the "right" way. Knowing yourself, your cultural bias, and the
emotional areas of your life most likely to cause stress can help
you anticipate your reactions.

Acceptance of self and transformation in Christ are especially
important if we hope to live and work between two cultural
worlds. Teaching cross-culturally works best when we accept
who we are and then embrace the necessity of change through
the power and grace of the Lord Jesus Christ. So if you want to
teach cross-culturally, welcome the adventure of cultural learning suggested throughout this book.

Research/Reflection Questions

1. If you have access to the Internet, find the official web site
   for the country you are going to or are in now. Locate other
   sites that contain information about the country's politics,
   history, population, literacy rates, life expectancies, and
   so on. How can you use this information in planning your
   classes?
2. Interview at least three missionaries to find out how they
   coped with culture shock. What reactions, if any, did they
   have in common? What can you learn from their stories?

References

Allen, Roland. 1930. *Missionary Methods, St. Paul's or Ours: A Study of the Church in Four Provinces.* London: World Dominion Press.

Bateson, Gregory. 1972. *Steps to an Ecology of Mind.* San Francisco: Chandler.

Berlin, Brent, and Paul Kay. 1969. *Basic Color Terms: Their Universality and Evolution.* Berkeley: University of California Press.

Bowen, Earle, and Dorthy. 1988. Contextualization of Teaching Methodology in Theological Education in Africa. ERIC Document Reproduction Service No. ED 315 382.

Brewster, Tom, and Elizabeth. 1976. *Language Acquisition Made Practical.* Colorado Springs: Lingua House.

Casse, Pierre. 1979. *Training for the Cross Cultural Mind.* Washington, D.C.: SIETAR.

Chinchen, Del. 1994. The Patron-Client Relationship Concept: A Case Study from the African Bible Colleges in Liberia and Malawi. Ph.D. diss., Biola University.

Cohen, Rosalie. 1969. Conceptual Styles, Culture Conflict, and Nonverbal Tests of Intelligence. *American Anthropologist* 71:828–56.

Douglas, Mary. 1982. Cultural Bias. In *In the Active Voice.* London: Routledge and Kegan Paul.

Dyrness, William A. 1990. *Learning about Theology from the Third World.* Grand Rapids: Zondervan.

Elmer, Duane. 1993. *Cross Cultural Conflict.* Downers Grove, Ill.: InterVarsity.

Farb, Peter. 1988. Man at the Mercy of Language. In *Toward Multiculturalism,* edited by Jaime S. Wurzel. Yarmouth, Maine: Intercultural Press.

Flowerdew, John, and Lindsay Miller. 1995. On the Notion of Culture in L2 Lectures. *TESOL Quarterly* 29, no. 2:345–73.

Furey, Patricia. 1986. A Framework for Cross-Cultural Analysis of Teaching Methods. In *Teaching Across Cultures in the University ESL Program,* edited by Patricia Byrd. Washington, D.C.: National Association for Foreign Student Affairs.

Gardner, Howard. 1983. *Frames of Mind: The Theory of Multiple Intelligences.* New York: Basic Books.

———. 1999. *Intelligence Reframed.* New York: Basic Books.

George, Pamela. 1995. *College Teaching Abroad.* Boston: Allyn and Bacon.

Gochenour, Theodore. 1993. *Beyond Experience.* 2d ed. Yarmouth, Maine: Intercultural Press.

Goodnow, Jacqueline. 1990. The Socialization of Cognition: What's Involved? In *Cultural Psychology: Essays on Comparative Human Development,* edited by James Stigler, Richard Shweder, and Gilbert Herdt. Cambridge: Cambridge University Press.

Harris, Stephen. 1984. *Culture and Learning.* Canberra, Australia: Institute for Aboriginal Studies.

Harvey, Jerry. 1988. *The Abilene Paradox.* New York: Lexington Books.

Heath, Shirley Brice. 1982. Questioning at Home and School: A Comparative Study. In *Doing the Ethnography of School-*

ing, edited by George Spindler. New York: Holt, Rinehart & Winston.

Henry, Jules. 1976. A Cross Cultural Outline of Education. In *Educational Patterns and Cultural Configurations,* edited by Joan Roberts and Sherrie Akinsanya. New York: David McKay.

Hiebert, Paul. 1982. The Flaw of the Excluded Middle. *Missiology* 10, no. 1:35–47.

Hilgard, Ernest, and Gordon Bower. 1981. *Theories of Learning.* 5th ed. Englewood Cliffs, N.J.: Prentice Hall.

Jackson, Philip. 1968. *Life in Classrooms.* New York: Holt, Rinehart & Winston.

Kohls, L. Robert, and John M. Knight. 1994. *Developing Intercultural Awareness: A Cross Cultural Training Handbook.* 2d ed. Yarmouth, Maine: Intercultural Press.

Kolb, David. 1984. *Experiential Learning.* Englewood Cliffs, N.J.: Prentice Hall.

Kraft, Charles H. 1983. *Communication Theory for Christian Witness.* Nashville: Abingdon.

———. 1999. *Communicating Jesus' Way.* Rev. ed. Pasadena, Calif.: William Carey Library.

Lewin, Kurt. 1957. Field Theory in Social Sciences. New York: Harper & Row.

Lingenfelter, Judith E. 1981. Schooling in Yap: Indigenization vs. Cultural Diversification. Ph.D. diss., University of Pittsburgh.

———. 1990. The Relationship between Cognitive Style and Schooling Success. *Christian Education Journal* (Hong Kong) 2:32–36.

Lingenfelter, Sherwood. 1992. *Transforming Culture.* Grand Rapids: Baker.

———. 1996. *Agents of Transformation.* Grand Rapids: Baker.

———. 1998. *Transforming Culture.* 2d ed. Grand Rapids: Baker.

Lingenfelter, Sherwood, and Marvin K. Mayers. 1986. *Ministering Cross-Culturally.* Grand Rapids: Baker.

Marantika, Saria. 2002. The Use of a Culturally Sensitive Song Form—Macapat—to Teach the Bible in Rural Java. Ph.D. diss., Biola University.

Mayers, Marvin K. 1987. *Christianity Confronts Culture*. 2d ed. Grand Rapids: Zondervan.

Murdock, George Peter. 1987. *Outline of Cultural Materials*. 5th rev. ed. New Haven, Conn.: Human Relations Area Files.

Ng, Tjoh Dju. 2000. A Study on Community at a Theological Institution in Manila Using Victor Turner's Theory. Ph.D. diss., School of Intercultural Studies, Biola University.

Oberg, Kalvero. 1960. Culture Shock: Adjustment to New Cultural Environments. *Practical Anthropology* 7:177–82.

Ouedraogo, Boureima, and Harriet Hill. 2002. When Bureaucracies Meet Relation-Based Organizations. *Ethno-info* no. 50 (March).

Piaget, Jean. 1970. *Science of Education and the Psychology of the Child*. New York: Viking.

Portin, Gail. 1993. Chinese Students and Questioning Skills in American Graduate Level Classrooms. M.A. thesis, Biola University.

Seelye, H. Ned. 1996. *Experiential Activities for Intercultural Learning*. Yarmouth, Maine: Intercultural Press.

Serpell, Robert. 1993. *The Significance of Schooling*. Cambridge: Cambridge University Press.

Spindler, George. 1987. *Education and Cultural Process*. 2d ed. Prospect Heights, Ill.: Waveland Press.

Steffen, Tom. 1996. *Reconnecting God's Story to Ministry: Cross-cultural Storytelling at Home and Abroad*. La Habra, Calif.: Center for Organization and Ministry Development.

Taylor, William, ed. 2000. *Global Missiology for the Twenty-First Century*. Grand Rapids: Baker.

Tobias, Cynthia. 1994. *The Way They Learn*. Wheaton: Tyndale.

Werner, David, and Bill Bower. 1982. *Helping Health Care Workers Learn*. Palo Alto, Calif.: Hesperian Foundation.

Wolcott, Harry. 1987. The Teacher as Enemy. In *Education and Cultural Process*, edited by George Spindler. 2d ed. Prospect Heights, Ill.: Waveland Press.

Index